It's Not Hard To Learn the Bard

A Guide to Introducing Shakespeare to Teenagers

Philip Schwadron

I dedicate this book to my twin brother Steven Schwadron, who played Benvolio in a 5th grade production of Romeo & Juliet. I've been chasing him ever since.

Also to every student I taught at the Orange County School of the Arts:
I learned as much as you did, and this book wouldn't have happened without you.

THE DIE IS CAST

I admit with pleasure that I am and have been a fan of William Shakespeare for nearly 20 years. For the last five years I have been fortunate enough to teach Shakespeare Appreciation at the Orange County School of the Arts, where I can exercise my right to fanboy all over the classroom every semester. Now I've taken it to the next level- the printed word! What I want to share with this book is how, as a teacher, I present this unnecessarily intimidating material to students, and how, as a student, one can easily learn this material using only two important parts of the body- the head and the heart. However, I have to say this book is not for Shakespearean scholars, nor am I encouraging any serious actors looking to join the Royal Shakespeare Company to consider this writing essential for their bookcase. There are plenty of schools and materials out there already for the advanced Bard fans. This book is for the rest of us, the regular kids from regular schools, the ones that may have an interest in acting or just studying the classics, but might be intimidated by his mighty reputation. Since Shakespeare wrote for regular people, and not just for the scholars to tear it apart 400 years later, we all have a right to know his work!

By the way, I was no different than the students I'm now teaching when it came to Julius Caesar and Romeo & Juliet. Those were the plays I was forced to study in 9th and 10th grade, and I do mean forced. I couldn't wait to be done with it, and didn't touch Shakespeare again for 15 years.

Remarkably, I completely avoided it in college, getting a degree in theatre arts from California State University, Northridge without taking a single Shakespeare class or performing in a single Shakespeare play. I was also concentrating on professional acting, and as we all know, Hollywood is about as interested in the classics as they are in movies with starring roles for women. In my 30s, things changed. Acting was out, and teaching was in. I started my second career as a substitute, and two of my first gigs were English classes where I had to teach Romeo & Juliet one day and MacBeth soon after that. I remember it like it was yesterday! I had a moment- an epiphany- where I realized I had a knack not only for understanding it but for explaining it. When I saw that the students responded positively, I was on my way. A year later I acted in A Midsummer Night's Dream at a community theater, and then in 2001 my graduate work began at the California Institute of the Arts MFA Acting program. Shakespeare was rightly a focus for the entire three-year program, and it began at a time when I finally felt ready to tackle the material. I played Leontes in Winter's Tale, Falstaff in Henry IV part one, Aguecheek in Twelfth Night, and Iachimo in Cymbeline. I became a huge fan of Shakespeare's work in those years, and it hasn't gone away. But really, it shouldn't have taken so long to get into his plays. My students over the years, mostly 11th graders, have made it clear to me I could have and should have been able to embrace Shakespeare at a young age, because they have. So what turned me off for so long? What turns most people off entirely? Well, I submit that the main reason for turning our backs on Shakespeare in modern America is simple: FEAR. What is it we fear? The obvious answer for both students and teachers is that we are afraid we won't understand it. And for people in my line of work, if we can't understand it, how can we teach it? As for the students, if the teacher is unsure, the students certainly will be. They'll smell the uncertainty. They're good at that. I began teaching Shakespeare at OCSA with my MFA at my back, knowing that I could help begin the process of accessing and digesting what Shakespeare is and what he has to offer. So this book is about a way into the world of the Bard, for teachers and students alike.

WHY?
First of all, the question needs to be asked: why should we teach Shakespeare at all? 400 year old plays? Confusing language? Kings and love sonnets? How could that possibly relate to the lives of Millennials? These kids, with their eyes glued to their cell phones, and their attention spans needing major improvement, couldn't possibly understand or even care about William

Shakespeare and that To Be or Not To Be nonsense, right?

Wrong.

Teenagers understand a few things that make Shakespeare not only worth teaching but relevant. For one thing, teens know about *longing* and *need* like no other age group. They long for love, for acceptance, for identity, and for knowledge. They need their peer groups. They need to talk about their lives. They need room to grow. If there's one poet/playwright who wrote about longing and need better than all others, it was William Shakespeare. Nobody ever, before or since, dug into the guts and soul of humanity with language so profound and beautiful. And we must use it to learn about ourselves. Shakespeare is our teacher. And that's what I tell my students on the first day of class.

LANGUAGE OUT

Let's start with a philosophical truth that often gets overlooked: Not much has changed since 1590. For that matter, not much has changed since 1090. Or 90. Or 1090 BC. We as human beings want to love and be loved, eat good food, make a living, and enjoy the arts. That goes back to Adam and Eve. So why would we think Shakespeare's characters are any different? But we do. We think they're smarter than us, deeper than us, and because they speak fancy, basically *not* us. But that's where we go wrong. Shakespeare was human; in fact he probably understood humanity better than most, and his characters therefore are very much human, and hence, very much us. So, I say that the first step in teaching Shakespeare (and I remind you I'm talking about the *first* step) is to take his words out of the discussion. There I said it. I know what you're thinking: run for your lives, the Philistines have entered the temple! But it's true. I haven't captured the interest of a single student with talk of iambic pentameter, rhyming couplets or symbolism. Instead, what grabs their attention during the first few days of class is a discussion about the obvious humanity and relatability of the characters. And the way to get to the humanity first is to shut off the fireworks of the language and see what is still there.

Take Romeo and Juliet for example. The play is *not* a love story. At least not if you remove the language and just follow the plot. It's about two teenagers trying to have sex without their parents finding out. Period. That's it. Sound familiar? It should. I have older brothers and sisters. I remember the trouble they got into when it came to bringing their significant others over while mom was out working an evening shift. Not much is different in Romeo & Juliet. They meet at a party where there's lots of young horny people. They make out about 30 seconds after they meet. They meet again later that night and make out some more. Then they make plans to meet again. Mom and Dad forbid it, because the families are in a fight. (Does this sound otherworldly? Sounds contemporary, actually.) So they sneak around behind the backs of their parents and get married (they're Catholic), but if you look closely at the marriage scene, they can't keep their hands off each other, and the Friar is trying to keep them separated long enough for them to say "I do". Then they go back to Juliet's room and consummate the marriage all night, with Romeo sneaking out the window before dawn. Like I said, they're human. And they're teenagers- impulsive and infatuated with each other. It all ends badly but that's because Juliet refuses to listen to her dad. More on that later.

Take the language out of Henry IV part one, and it's a play about a son and his disapproving father, nothing more. Prince Hal is hanging out at the bar with a bunch of drinking buddies who like to tell bad jokes, sleep with women, and steal. King Henry is worried about holding the throne, and even if he can, what will happen to England with this loser son of his next in line. I know my students can relate to Hal. Based on the stories they tell me about their lives, I also know they think their parents can relate to King Henry. It breaks my heart but it just proves that nothing has changed.

As You Like It minus language becomes a play about a very smart young woman who has a good time messing with the boy she likes. Modern? You'd better believe it. Rosalind, disguised as a boy, makes her crush, who happens to be crushing hard on her too, rehearse his poetic pick up lines to this Rosalind girl with Rosalind! Orlando, the boy, doesn't know it's Rosalind he's rehearsing with, so he clumsily goes along with it. It's a fantasy most every modern girl has, to eavesdrop on her boyfriend's mind! So the play holds up nicely, and the big reveal at the end, when Orlando realizes he's been talking to Rosalind the whole time, still makes a nice impact.

In one of the most famous opening monologues in theatre history, Richard III makes it clear that really he just can't get laid, so he schemes to take the throne instead. He says now that the wars are over, the men, instead of fighting battles, are all in bedrooms having sex with the ladies. But Richard is deformed and ugly, with a hunchback, withered right arm, and a clubbed foot, so no one will touch him. Therefore, instead of messing around with women, he will be a villain, manipulate his brothers against each other, and eventually take the crown for himself. Everything that happens is driven by thoughts from this first speech, and all that first speech is about is sexual frustration, and what he's going to do about it. Richard says:

And therefore, since I cannot prove a lover
To entertain these fair well-spoken days,
I am determinèd to prove a villain
And hate the idle pleasures of these days.
Plots have I laid, inductions dangerous,
By drunken prophecies, libels and dreams,
To set my brother Clarence and the king
In deadly hate, the one against the other

If Richard III had a girlfriend when the war ended, there would be no play.

By now I assume you see where I'm going with this concept. Yes, of course the language is the emphatic element of Shakespeare, and always will be, because it's some of the most beautiful and emotionally impacting language ever written for the stage or anywhere else. But that's for later. Believe it or not, it's just the icing on the cake. Really *really* good icing, but not the cake. The cake is the humanity of the characters. If we don't relate to them on a purely gut level, the language is nothing. We must start by seeing ourselves in them. Take Hamlet, Othello, and Lady MacBeth off the pedestals they have been falsely put on and make them just like us. Because they are. Hamlet is emo, Othello is jealous, and Lady MacBeth is manipulative. Once the story and characters are clear, put the language back in and you'll see how beautiful it truly is. But you have to know what's going on with the story before the language can be understood and appreciated.

One word of caution: beware of false prophets. In the last 15 years a series called "No Fear Shakespeare" started showing up in bookstores. I see the students reading through them, and it discourages me. I think the series is nothing more than a cheater's guide; a cheap substitute for the real thing. It's got the actual text on the left side and a "modern translation" on the right. That bugs me more than I can say. First of all, you can't translate from English to English. That's absurd. Plus, since it does the work for you, why even bother looking at the left side when you have to have it read by tomorrow along with the other six hours of homework demanded every day? The most important reason I reject the series, however, is that it assumes you're not smart enough or intuitive enough to do the interpreting of the poetry on your own. In other words, it assumes you're dumb. Don't accept that assumption. Of course you're smart enough. Shakespeare wrote this stuff for you. The irony of the whole thing is the title "No Fear Shakespeare" does the opposite. It keeps you afraid of it.

HOW MANY?!!
There are 37 plays in the Shakespeare canon, written in a span of only about 20 years, I might add, 1590-1610. This man wrote fast and furiously, and then retired at age 47! Unlike many other famous artists, the ones who starved and whose work wasn't appreciated until after their deaths, Shakespeare was writing hits during his lifetime. He knew how to create plays that got butts in seats, as they say, and he made good money. He made enough at the end of his career to buy land back in Stratford,his hometown, and there died in 1616 at age 52. That's a young age. Just imagine if he had

a 30 year career instead of 20! Although, I believe most of the world's greatest artists have about a ten year window of doing great work, and then spend the remainder of their careers living off their reputations. I do not say that to slam the artists nor the art, because an artist should keep creating without worrying about such things. It's just a simple fact that if you take the best music acts, the best playwrights, and the best filmmakers, there will be a period of time where they can do no wrong and churn out success after success, but it's only about ten years, and then they just tour playing those hits or revive those plays over and over again. That's the nature of art, in my opinion. Each unique gift is finite, which is ok. Ten years obviously can create a lot of good work, and of course there are plenty of very special careers that still create something fresh 20-30 years in, like Neil Young, Quentin Tarantino and Stephen Sondheim, among others. Shakespeare should also be in that very special category. Among his early plays were Richard III and Romeo & Juliet, and his final works were The Winter's Tale and The Tempest. Not bad! At the beginning of each semester, the students can name maybe 7 plays by Shakespeare, on average. I know because I quiz them on Day One. And in almost every class, it's the same basic five that actually pop into all of our heads, even us grown ups, when we're asked to name titles by the Bard: Romeo & Juliet, Hamlet, A Midsummer Night's Dream, Julius Caesar, and MacBeth.

There's one or two others that vary from student to student (and adult to adult), like Richard III, Othello, Much Ado About Nothing, Twelfth Night, and The Merry Wives of Windsor. I must say I notice Cyrano de Bergerac gets mentioned a lot, but I forgive them for that; it's a good guess and the right period in history, even though Rostand wrote it only 120 years ago!

My favorite plays are none of these, however, and I love introducing students to the lesser known works, because each monologue I hand out from these more obscure titles gets a plot summary by me, so they are absorbing around 20 plays per semester, most of them they've never heard of, rather than the typical 5 we all know. Let the regular academics expose them to Julius Caesar and MacBeth. They get Cymbeline, Titus Andronicus, Henry V and Measure For Measure from me. Some of those plays leave a more lasting impact, in my opinion, than the five to seven usual suspects.

By the way, all those great titles doesn't mean they're *all* great titles. I've been asked many times if every one of Shakespeare's plays are sacred classics. Absolutely not. Of his 37 plays, at least 20 deserve to be performed and studied forever. That leaves 17 that aren't as good, and out of those, maybe 4 or 5 that can disappear entirely, in my opinion. Yes, even the greatest geniuses had a few clunkers. King John, Troilus and Cressida, King Henry VIII and Pericles do nothing for me. They may have their fans, but I'm sure Tennesee Williams had fans who found worth in "Clothes for a Summer Hotel". Doesn't mean it's any good.

THE CLASSROOM VERSUS THE STAGE.
First off, let's be clear- Shakespeare is a poet. There is absolute good in studying his works as literature in a high school English Literature class. No doubt about that. It deserves to be there. But although that was the original intent of the sonnets, it was not for the plays. Theatre was, theatre is, and theatre always will be meant to be spoken and heard, not read for homework or analyzed for an entire semester. His language is much easier to understand when listening to it, and is actually quite annoying for many to read. Even when read out loud in class it's a problem, as modern students struggle with his sentence structure, which seems to be all over the place at first glance. The reason for that is back in the 1590s, the English language was still fairly new. There were a few rules in place but nowhere near the rules we're taught today and use in everyday speech. Those rules simply didn't exist, so the language was much more free for Shakespeare to shape as he needed to. It doesn't naturally relate to the modern ear, any more than Beethoven does. But also like Beethoven, once you get into it, it's hard to get out.
So how does one get into it? Well, in spite of the very horror with which the words are accompanied when the teacher says them, we should start with

Iambic Pentameter. No student wants to spend more than five seconds on what it means or how you speak it, so here is a five second explanation: Iambic is unstressed/stressed. Penta means five, and Meter is line. So, there are five unstressed/stressed beats per line. The end. What students do understand instinctively is exactly what the iambic pentameter does, and therefore, of course, why Shakespeare was such a genius for using it: it mimics a heartbeat. Ba BUM. Ba BUM. Ba BUM. It's a very human rhythm. Pick a line and try it. I'll use Malcolm's speech in MacBeth:

*Hence**forth** be **earls**, the **first** that **ever Scot**land*
*In **such** an **hon**our **nam'd**. What's **more** to **do**,*
*Which **would** be **plant**ed **new**ly **with** the **time**, —*
*As **call**ing **home** our **exil**'d **friends** a**broad**,*
*That **fled** the **snares** of **watch**ful **tyr**anny;*

Do you hear the heartbeat? That's Iambic Pentameter. Lesson Complete.

I have found over the years that once a student approaches the heartbeat idea, they forget about word placement and get into the rhythm. Even better, there are some lines where the iambic is inverted, meaning it's stressed and then unstressed (***Now** is the **win**ter of our **dis**con**tent**).* Think about what happens if the heart suddenly beats in reverse. It's startling, and, of course, probably fatal, but the point is the break up of the rhythm is used for dramatic effect. So once again, I say the drama is in the language. The Iambic Pentameter also keeps the students from doing a very student thing, which is rushing through the speech as fast as they can, so they can sit down as quickly as possible with their dignity still intact. I coach them as much as I can to slow down and feel the tempo dramatically. Is the character angry? In love? Anxious? The mood sets the tempo, like in a song. A rock and roll party song is an upbeat tempo, a sad jazzy breakup song is slower. This is also how to memorize it. Remember, Shakespeare was an actor, and understood the actor's need to memorize lines quickly. Iambic Pentameter is the tool he gave them to memorize. Here's what I tell the students: why is learning song lyrics easier than memorizing dialogue? Is it because it rhymes? Of course, but it's also because it's in a rhythm. Arranging syllables to match the beat is how songwriting works, and Shakespeare wrote his dialogue like songs. When you think about it, he was a 16th century rap artist! We memorize song lyrics faster than dialogue because of the beat, so Shakespeare was giving his actors a big advantage over other playwrights of the period (or any period for that matter!) I suggest to the students to use the iambics to memorize. See how it scans, stay in that rhythm, and you'll instinctively start rapping it which makes it easier to memorize. It works!

One other thing about speaking the speech: Don't worry about using a "Shakespeare voice." I can't tell you how many times a student has been handed a monologue or scene and then asks me "Do you want me to try it with a British accent?" As if the final polish of a Shakespearean performance is to sound like an Englishman! Nothing against our former mother country, but nothing could be further from the truth. In reality, when Shakespeare was writing, the British accent as we know it was not a British accent. It didn't exist. Brits had an accent more like the famous pirate accents of Captain Barbossa in "Pirates of the Caribbean" and Long John Silver in "Treasure Island". In the 1700s the German Hannover family took over the British throne, and the accent that is today's British began to take shape thanks to the Hannovers' German accent. In other words, in Shakespeare's time, the British accent was closer to modern American than modern British, so you won't score points with me by sounding "British" when acting Shakespeare. In fact you'll lose points. At Cal Arts, I was taught a Standard American Classical accent, which is really easy if you're from the east coast, which I am (Atlantic City, New Jersey. Go Vikings!). But really, your own regional accent will do just fine. Speak normal, guys. We're listening for the meaning and drama, not the accent.

MODERN ISSUES

One way to get students to relate to this material is to pick out the contemporary issues that Shakespeare tackled 400 years ago. Whatever can get them hooked into the material is fair game. A lengthy discussion on the subject involves first the issues themselves, which can take anywhere from a few minutes to almost the entire class period, which is fine with me if the discussion feels like we're hitting on something important. Next would be examples of how the 16th century saw the issues and which characters embodied them. Some of the social issues that Shakespeare wrote about include the following:

SEXISM

Women in Shakespeare's time were not allowed to perform on stage. It took 44 years after Shakespeare's death for a woman to act in a theatre. (FYI-The first recorded female actor in England was Margaret Hughes, who played Desdemona in a production of *Othello* on December 8, 1660. Charles II must be thanked for finally knocking down that law!) But how did Shakespeare feel about women? I'm inclined to believe that he saw them as at least equals, and in many cases as intellectual and moral superiors. The evidence exists in the plays. Look at Queen Margaret from the history plays, look at Hermione from Winter's Tale, look at Rosalind from As You Like It. Hell, look at Juliet- A fourteen year old girl in the late 16th century telling her father in no uncertain terms: "I will not marry the man you command me to marry. I will not obey you. I want Romeo, and if I can't have Romeo, I'm leaving this world." And she meant it. I can't imagine the shockwaves this must have sent through society in

1593! She defied her father and lived her life on her own terms. Bold, nuclear bomb stuff!

I should mention at this point the cross-dressing device. So many of Shakespeare's plays involved females dressed as boys. There were a few reasons for this: first, cross dressing has been a staple of comedy for 500 years at least. Just ask Bugs Bunny. Another reason was that since women couldn't be on stage, their roles were played by boys or young men, so getting the young men back in men's clothes made things easy when the audience was asked to believe nobody saw through the disguise. But the third reason for the cross dressing is the most important- I think Shakespeare did it because the only way the other male characters would listen to this woman's ideas was to not know it was a woman. If that possibly sexist point of view doesn't work for you, look at it this way: Shakespeare gave his women characters intellect equal to the men, and the opportunity to express their intellect freely that they wouldn't have had if the men knew they were talking to women. I think it shows that Shakespeare wanted his audience to understand how smart and mature women were if they were able to live in a man's world. Bold stuff again! Also, keep this in mind: when Shakespeare hit the London scene, there was a woman on the throne, the remarkable monarch Elizabeth I. The last and greatest member of the Tudor dynasty that began with Henry VII's defeat of Richard III in 1485, Elizabeth, luckily, was a great lover of the theatre. Her influence on his depiction of women characters can't be understated. Up until her death in 1603, Shakespeare had the support of his queen to write and produce theatre to his heart's content. A blessing to us all. By the way, when James I began his reign upon Elizabeth's death in 1603, he wasn't the theatre arts patron that Elizabeth was, but he didn't shut it down either. Shakespeare wrote plenty of winners in the last 7 years of his career under King James.

There is, unfortunately, one particular play of Shakespeare's that I have not been able to reconcile with modern feminist sensibility- The Taming of the Shrew. I tried. I attempted to discuss the play, and once or twice showed my students the Richard Burton/Elizabeth Taylor film from 1967 with a second discussion of the play afterwards, but the reaction by the class was Petruchio was "rapey". And they were right. He's abusive and harmful to Kate and her psyche. Maybe she's being a baby, but that's different than evil, and the damage to her soul, in my opinion, is unfunny. There are some wonderful scenes where it's clearly an equal battle of the sexes, both characters having discovered they met their match. But then he treats her so horribly in the other scenes, the ones at his house- keeping her from eating, cutting up her dress, locking her in a room all night, not to mention the final speech of the play where she swears obedience to her lord and master because that's what love apparently is, that I decided to leave it out of my class from then on. Right or wrong, that's what I did. There was plenty of material that held up better after 400 years.

That famous episode of the 1980s tv show "Moonlighting" deserves mention here. "Atomic Shakespeare", based on Taming of the Shrew, was a classic moment in television history, at the time the most expensive episode ever filmed. The show as a whole was a modern battle of the sexes, so Taming of the Shrew was a natural way to go for these characters. And the whole episode was written in Iambic Pentameter, which is pretty impressive. The ending takes a modern liberal view of sexual equality, with Petruccio declaring you can get more from your wife by "holding her at thy side, rather than under thy thumb." I've shown it many times, most recently in 2015. It holds up! The kids laugh a lot. You can find it on DVD. Just saying.

I actually played Kate in college in a "line-reversal" performance. We didn't switch genders, just lines. So I was literally tied up and dragged to the church by a woman (good times!). I do think that was and is a good way to deal with the sexism in the play- let the woman be the dominator. I think it gives the audience the right perspective on the comedy. It makes it funny again. It's the same reason (actually one of many) that the Broadway musical "Hamilton" works so well- it's the story of America's beginning told by today's Americans, rather than just the white men who were dominant back then. When we see ourselves, the story stays relevant.

RACISM
Let's talk about Othello. The students first need to understand the fact that Othello is not black as we understand the term in the 21st century. Othello is a Moor, a Spanish African Muslim. In the 9th century Muslim Africans made their way across the Mediterranean to Spain. The Moorish culture that developed there was sophisticated for its time (and much of the art and architecture of the Moors still exists in Spain. It's spectacular!), so the idea that a Moor wound up a military general in Venice is not so far fetched. But Othello's wife was white. An interracial marriage in 1600 is pretty bold, but as I've been emphasizing all along, if Shakespeare is anything, he is bold. But is the play racist? Iago certainly has plenty of racist descriptions of Othello when he awakens Desdemona's father with the news the she and Othello have eloped:

IAGO
Even now, now, very now, an old black ram
Is tupping your white ewe. Arise, arise!
Awake the snorting citizens with the bell,
Or else the devil will make a grandsire of you.

There is other dialogue about Othello being dark, but in Shakespeare's time that could also be any European with tan skin. In Henry VI part 1, Joan La

Pucelle, better known as Joan of Arc, calls herself "black and swart" from being out in the sun all day while tending sheep. And she is clearly white. The real racism of Othello, in my opinion, occurs externally, because for hundreds of years, all the way into the late 20th century, white actors played the role in blackface!

But in the play itself, I give Shakespeare credit. While Othello is described by his enemies as a beast and less than human, Shakespeare makes him very human. The real feeling of being isolated and different comes from within Othello himself. I think he buys Iago's lies so easily because he always knew he wasn't good enough for Desdemona. The rest of his actions and reactions are nothing more than pure pride and male ego. His manhood is on the line, like any one's would be when his wife is cheating. However, he has no speech about "We should all be equal", like Shylock has in Merchant of Venice. Othello is another one of the plays I avoid teaching or viewing, because I just don't like it. I think Othello is a bastard. He treats his wife horribly, and it's his own insecurity that brings out his jealousy which then leads to his murder of her. Iago is a blowhard, driven by nothing but hate. Even Desdemona, the only noble character in the whole thing, blames herself in her death speech, which is crap. Luckily in this modern time, my experience has been that the students don't stand for behavior like this, nor should they.

By the way, I studied Othello in an Advanced Placement English class my senior year in high school. I couldn't sit with the idea that Shakespeare wrote a play where jealousy lead to the murder of an innocent woman. What's the point of that? I told my teacher in that class that I wanted to grab Othello by the collar and yell "HE'S LYING!!!! CAN'T YOU SEE IAGO IS LYING??!!! LEAVE HER ALONE!!" She actually gave me permission to re-write the ending as a project. I wouldn't dream of creating new dialogue, but I did present a plot summary of the new ending- Othello doesn't kill anyone in my version. Iago is found out as a liar before Othello reaches Desdemona's bedroom that night. He has Iago arrested and offers a heartfelt apology to his wife. In graduate school I discovered there's a similar ending to my re-worked Othello in The Winter's Tale, where King Leontes has an opportunity to reconcile with and apologize to his wife, Queen Hermione, for his jealousy and all it has cost him. It makes me wonder if Shakespeare was apologizing to his audiences for the ending of Othello with the ending of Winter's Tale. I bet he was! Something tells me he was constantly trying to make a better play. The only other characters of color in Shakespeare's plays that are large enough to be worth mentioning are Aaron in Titus Andronicus and Caliban in The Tempest. Aaron is also a Moor like Othello, but his character is not motivated by jealousy or pride. He was just taking revenge on the people that conquered him, and offers no real depth of motivation in his final scene, just that he enjoyed it. (Aaron is asked "*Art thou not sorry for these heinous deeds?*" He replies "*Ay, that I had not done a thousand more*".) He does, however, father a mixed race baby with Tamora, the Queen of the Goths, and saves the baby at the end.

Caliban from The Tempest is a native of the island that Prospero the magician lives on, but his nationality is never mentioned since the island is purely Shakespeare's invention. However, he is a slave, and treated as subhuman by Prospero. Also there are those that believe that he is based on Native Americans. It is true that Native Americans would have been to London a few times by 1610 (the British colony of Jamestown was established in 1607, during Shakespeare's final years in the theatre), and I happen to think it's probably true that Jamestown and Indians were on his mind as he wrote the play, but there's no way to know for sure. Today's students, however, are more aware of Native American history than previous generations, so it always excites them to think Shakespeare has a Native American character. Whatever gets them hooked works for me.

ANTI-SEMITISM

Jews were not thought of highly in Shakespeare's time. In the mindset of the day, they weren't going to heaven, and they were Jesus killers. In the play Merchant of Venice, the Jews practiced usury, which is the lending of money with interest, which was against Christian law. But since Jews couldn't own their own businesses they had no choice. So the stereotype of Jews being conservative with money was created by oppression by the Christians. Irony.

Shakespeare, however, does give Shylock a beautiful speech about equality, and thus he is a much fuller human character than other Jewish characters of Shakespeare's day. It's famously known as the "Hath not a Jew eyes" speech:

SHYLOCK
I am a Jew. Hath not a Jew eyes? Hath not a Jew hands,
organs, dimensions, senses, affections, passions; fed with the same
food, hurt with the same weapons, subject to the same diseases,
heal'd by the same means, warm'd and cool'd by the same winter
and summer, as a Christian is? If you prick us, do we not bleed? If
you tickle us, do we not laugh? If you poison us, do we not die?
And if you wrong us, do we not revenge?

Notice the speech is not in verse. Shakespeare saved verse for the noble characters, or at least for when the lower characters spoke nobly. For this famous speech, Shakespeare give Shylock prose, not verse. That says something about the opinion of Jews in the 16th century.

Christopher Marlowe's The Jew of Malta is a jew of pure revenge and murder, and the play is unapologetic in its depiction of Barabas as rich and evil. The Merchant of Venice is actually a comedy, with most of the other characters involved in the story either romantic lovers or comic servants. In the 1600s, Shylock's forced conversion to Christianity at the end of the trial scene would have been considered a happy moment for the audience. A Jew becoming a Christian would mean he's going to heaven, and Shylock's daughter Jessica already has already run away with Lorenzo and converted. Today we see Shylock as a tragic figure trapped in a comedy. Shylock goes too far in demanding a pound of flesh, and his conversion is the price he pays. He is brought down by his own hubris. The students have a very difficult time understanding how Shylock comes up with such a crazy idea as taking a pound of flesh. What I tell them is yes, he's nuts. But it's not because he's Jewish, it's because he's angry at Antonio for spitting on him and clearly overreacts. They have replied in the past "oh it's like those crazy guys who get fired and come back and shoot their boss." Yes. Something like that. There are other lines from Shakespeare's plays, like Benedick's line from Much Ado About Nothing: "If I do not love her, I am a Jew" that may show Shakespeare to be an anti Semite, but it's also true that Thomas Jefferson said "All men are created equal" while owning slaves. If we can forgive Jefferson for being stuck in a difficult time while still having a vision of equality, we can read Shakespeare's Hath not a Jew Eyes speech, understand the times he was living in, and also understand that Shakespeare was a humanist before the word was coined, and we can make a few adjustments for modern times. Joss Whedon politely changed Benedick's line to "If I do not love her, I am a *fool*" for his film version of Much Ado About Nothing in 2012.

HOMOSEXUALITY

Homosexuality has obviously existed since humans walked upright, but in Shakespeare's day it was not talked about nor represented on stage. But in a strange twist of irony to the complete secrecy of homosexuals in 16th century society, the laws that forbade women from performing in the theatre left it up to men and young boys to play female roles. In short, Elizabethan theatre, among the many other things it was, was also a drag show!

There are no openly gay characters in Shakespeare's plays. That would have been impossible legally and socially in the late 16th century. Shakespeare would have been arrested for it, and ostracised as well. But still, like every other art form of the time, there were hints.

For example, in As You Like It, Rosalind flees to the forest and disguises herself as a boy. The name she chooses for her fake identity is

Ganymede. Anyone who studies Greek mythology knows that Ganymede was abducted by Zeus to be his cup-bearer and boy lover. Erotic relationships between adult males and adolescent boys was accepted in ancient Greek society, so Shakespeare letting Rosalind give herself the name of Ganymede was clearly an inside joke that educated men would have understood!

In Twelfth Night, the character of Sir Andrew Aguecheek is interesting to me. I played the role at Cal Arts, and I noticed from the text that he was awkward with women, interested in fashion and dance, and most importantly, alone. I realized this guy was a stock "sissy" character, the kind that Hollywood was famous for using in the era of the Hayes Code, a time of censorship to keep movies tasteful from the 1930s through the early 60s. These sissy characters were effeminate but not overtly so, and clearly not masculine either. Today we wouldn't tolerate such ambiguity. We would rightly demand a character like that identify with his orientation. But in Shakespeare's day, the best he could come up with was Aguecheek, who was technically a heterosexual, but clearly just not very good at it! He does have a line about being "*a fellow o' th' strangest mind i' th' world. I delight in masques and revels sometimes altogether*". A "strange mind" could be code for the obvious. Then there's this line Aguecheek says, which hits us over the head with metaphor about as subtly as a runaway locomotive: "*I am a great eater of beef, and I believe that does harm to my wit*" Feel free to draw your own conclusion, but I think the evidence is there.

Also in Twelfth Night, Viola is dressed as a boy to deliver a love poem to Olivia, who promptly falls for her (him). Viola's reaction makes it clear she'll love no woman ("poor lady, she were better love a dream"). But that kind of hint, of Viola considering, for a moment, if she could love Olivia, is as close to lesbianism as Shakespeare gets. It simply wasn't represented in the plays other than for comic effect.

POLITICS

High school students can't vote, and sometimes I'm grateful about that (there are times I look at my students and realize the only difference between 10th graders and 3rd graders is that the 10th graders are taller). But the truth is they're more politically savvy than we give them credit for. They understand the social issues out there, everything from gay rights and transgender bathrooms to terrorism and immigration. More importantly, they certainly recognize a crooked politician when they see one. Our current presidential election year (2016), I must say, has given the students quite a colorful cast of characters to compare to Shakespeare's kings (and without a doubt also the clowns!). What makes a great leader and what makes a bad one are common themes in Shakespeare's history plays, and the crop of candidates running for president this year are quite

Shakespearean. Richard III, the epitome of the evil, ambitious, manipulative power grabber, is certainly a character that the students can relate to today's politicians. Some say it's Hillary Clinton, others Donald Trump (I still say it's Nixon). Richard II was the vain, self-loving, reckless monarch that some will compare to Bernie Sanders and others to Donald Trump. Henry V, the triumphant war king and inspirational leader, can be President Obama or Donald Trump. King Lear? Donald Trump. Lear's fool? Donald Trump. Yes, Trump is many things to many people. Which brings me to a word of warning- some students very much like discussing politics, but others do not and get very upset when they hear the true opinions of their friends on certain issues. I always try to instill a civil tone, but with the maturity levels low (in some cases; in other cases the maturity levels are as good as any worthy adult), I have been asked several times by my school's boss to stop discussing such things! Too bad, because I think it's important to keep the soon-to-be-electorate informed and armed with a few learned debate skills.

But back to the politicians of Shakespeare's works. The ones that I actually like best are the ones a little harder to figure out. Antony and Cleopatra, for example, is a great play about middle-aged lovers set against the backdrop of war between Rome and Egypt. Antony is a previously exalted general who now is in his 50s and lazily having a love affair with the queen of Egypt. He shirks his duties and lives off his reputation until Octavius back home in Rome calls him on it and then brings his army to defeat him. Cleopatra, meanwhile, nearly 40 herself, stays out of these Roman quarrels, preferring to live in splendor and sleep with Anthony when he's available, and not do much else. She shows her backbone, however, when she refuses to be displayed as a war trophy in Rome, and kills herself instead, after Antony's defeat and death. It's hard to pick a modern politician who resembles this kind of lazy war general and his monarch girlfriend. Eisenhower was the last general to be president. He certainly wasn't lazy, just old. Bill Clinton was sleeping with other women while president, but his actions started an impeachment trial, not a war. In any case, take their occupations away from Antony and Cleopatra and we have two very human characters going through mid-life crises. Shakespeare, by the way, was probably 45 when he wrote it, so I think it's interesting that as he aged, so did the characters he was writing. Prospero, the older man in The Tempest, was soon to follow Antony & Cleopatra.

Hamlet has always been a play with a political central theme, in my opinion. We're talking about the assassination of a king, and his throne being occupied by his next-in-line scheming brother and unsuspecting widow. Yes, Hamlet himself is just a grieving son who doesn't know how to get into the revenge business, but the play begins with a pretty catastrophic political event. Someone could write a whole new modern movie based on the idea of an American President being assassinated, and the murder ordered by his Vice President. Think of it! And of course, there's The Lion King, the Disney movie with the Hamlet plot- Brother kills brother and takes his throne. The similarities between the movie and the play actually stop there, but the percentage of students who have seen The Lion King is much higher than the percentage that has seen Hamlet, so I like to mention it. Whatever peaks their interest!

MODERN TECHNOLOGY
No point in denying it- cell phones and smartphones may be no more than a toy in the hands of of Millennials, but it's also their greatest tool. Yes, they sneak pictures of me for their Snapchat, and before I know it I'm turned into a rabbit and it's sent around the school by the time of the first passing bell. But they also use their phones to take notes, store papers, share information on classes, and look things up. So let's not fight it. I share with them that there is a an app on my phone called Shakespeare Complete. It has every play he wrote or co-wrote, every sonnet, and every poem, plus a dictionary and a Shakespeare search engine. It's awesome! I also enjoy an app called iTunes U, which is a library of podcasts from all over the world. There you'll find plenty of Shakespearean scholars discussing Shakespeare things, including one series from my favorite

museum, The Huntington Library and Botanical Gardens in San Marino, California. Also in 2016, for the 400th anniversary of Shakespeare's death (April 23, 1616), the great British actor Sir Ian McKellan launched the first of a series of 37 apps for the ipad that features each play, called Heuristic Shakespeare's iTunes. Full text, videos of scenes read and discussed by Mr. McKellan and others, plus historical notes, scene breakdowns, and just about everything you want. Let them know about it, there might be a few who look it up!

ANOTHER TEEN MOVIE
Hollywood got in the Shakespeare game in late 1990's and early 2000's. You may remember a slew of films that clearly had Shakespeare's plots, and by a not-so-strange coincidence they all took place in high schools. "Ten Things I Hate About You" (Taming of the Shrew), "She's the Man" (Twelfth Night), "O" (Othello), and "Get Over It" (A Midsummer Night's Dream). When I bring up these films, the students always have seen them or at least know of them, but had *no idea* they're based on Shakespeare plays! That drives me crazy, because it means the films weren't marketed as having Shakespeare-based material, which is a waste of an opportunity to bring an entire generation into contact with the Bard. The studios have an interesting dilemma I suppose in that they, along with so many others, clearly think Shakespeare equals "Boring." That doesn't really

surprise me, of course, because Hollywood is run by 12 year-old boys in 35 year-old bodies who wouldn't know art if it jumped in their faces with a machine gun next to a hot chick in tight leather who needed saving. And yet, these films were greenlighted, shot and released. Is it possible the writers pulled a fast one and never told the producers about the source material? I guess that's not my concern. My issue is the kids love these films and are totally engrossed in the characters and plots. All that tells me is I'm on the right track about not focusing on the language at first when teaching students. The other issue about the teen films I find interesting is why teens? Petruchio and Kate are not teenagers in Shakespeare's play. Othello is not high school age. Why set them in high school? My hunch is that Shakespeare's natural emotionalism inherent in his works is only believable in the modern age when experienced by teens. Adults in America have been conditioned to avoid emotions at best and repress them at worst, which is a tragedy of course. We'd have less anger if were allowed to express all the other emotions that anger is covering for. That's my opinion, but it's based partly from the things we're talking about, that only teens are seen as able to experience such heightened emotionalism. Ten Things I Hate About You is actually a good film, mainly because Julia Styles and the late great Heath Ledger are truly talented actors. My students actually talked me into watching She's the Man (after I showed them a version of the actual Twelfth Night). I wish I had those two hours back. I say no more about that. "O" I saw once and still haven't seen "Get Over It", which so far I don't regret. But the thing I do regret is Hollywood is clearly in cahoots with the anti-Shakespeare crowd. In any case, my advice is don't let students talk you into showing modern teen adaptations of Shakespeare plays. The plots are only part of the experience. The language of course is the ultimate element they need to absorb, otherwise it's not Shakespeare.

Which brings me to Baz Luhrman's Romeo + Juliet. Every year the students ask me to watch that one, and every year I say no. I hate the movie. Now, let me preface this by saying I like Baz Luhrman's other movies. Moulin Rouge is a classic! Strictly Ballroom is also a wonderful film. But this one he got wrong. Why? Because the emphatic element of every single one of Shakespeare's plays is *language*. It will always be language. The drama is in the language. The objective, the through-line, the super objective, and all those other terms I learned from my years in professional acting is in the language when it's Shakespeare. Baz Luhrman made the emphatic element the visuals. I reject that. Visuals are nice, editing is nice, but this is Shakespeare. Language is what it's all about. Call me a purist but to me it's true. So here's the final scene in Luhrman's movie: A beautiful looking tomb. A body in white. Candles. Lots of candles.

Candlelight bouncing off Romeo's silver costume. And there's Romeo, saying his farewell and drinking the poison. He dies as Juliet awakes. She cries, but says nothing, then picks up the gun, and shoots herself. I say again- *she says nothing.* He took away her entire final speech. Shakespeare's text is not reduced, but gone. I call shenanigans on that decision.

The Franco Zeffirelli film "Romeo and Juliet" from 1968 holds up well, but when it comes to the famous star-crossed lovers, I like to show my students "Shakespeare in Love". It's one of my all time favorite films! Clever dialogue, wonderful acting, and a love of Shakespeare's language by the characters as well as the actual writers of the screenplay, Tom Stoppard and Marc Norman. By the end of the semester my students know enough about the subject matter that they recognize all the Shakespearean references in the film- the girl in boy's clothes, the accusing ghost, a balcony scene, plus all the actual history of the period. Every time I show it they love it, I'm happy to say.

The other films I tend to show in class are Kenneth Branagh's "Henry V" (they recognize all the Harry Potter actors and a 13 year-old Christian Bale), Joss Whedon's "Much Ado About Nothing", and Michael Radford's "Merchant of Venice" with Al Pacino and Jeremy Irons. I wasn't sure about "Henry V", because in my school most of the classes are predominately female, and "Henry V" is all about men in big heavy armor marching to

France in the rain to fight. The first time I showed it they only liked that unique scene that's completely in French with Emma Thompson playing the French princess that Henry will marry. Recently, though, the students have warmed up to it and it keeps their attention very well. Plus, that incredible continuous 5 minute shot after the battle of Agincourt is a classic!

"The Merchant of Venice" is a dark film with dark humor, and Pacino plays Shylock as a man with no humor at all. He is completely depressing to watch, but as it turns out he's saving it for the Hath Not a Jew Eyes speech. The whole cast does a wonderful job, and the trial scene alone makes the entire movie worth watching. Whedon's "Much Ado About Nothing" is also very well-acted, and although those California accents drive me crazy, nobody else ever notices. Shot in black and white at Whedon's own home in only twelve days, he gets the most out of the location and his performers, particularly Nathan Fillion as Dogberry and Clark Gregg as Leonato.

I tried showing Al Pacino's "Looking for Richard", which is a documentary and a personal favorite of mine, but they were frustrated with Pacino moving in and out of actual scenes from Richard III and scenes of the actors rehearsing in street clothes or Pacino just talking about the play with famous Shakespeare people. It's possible that they just don't recognize a lot of the famous actors and directors in it, like John Gielgud and Peter Brook, and so it doesn't hold up as well.

I want to mention here that there's a DVD series from PBS called Shakespeare Uncovered, a wonderful recent collection of 90-minute episodes with famous movie actors who have played Shakespeare's greatest characters, and scholars who have taught and studied the Bard. They tackle the great plays, one or two per episode- *Hamlet* with David Tennant, *King Lear* with Christopher Plummer, *Twelfth Night* and *As You Like It* with Joely Richardson, and *Henry IV* and *Henry V* with Jeremy Irons. They talk history, text analysis, and show clips of famous movie and tv versions of the plays. Two seasons so far, 6 episodes per season. I've shown several episodes during the last few years, and I hope they keep it going!

Although this book is not a study in film criticism, I'm bringing up movies because let's face it, teachers can't afford to take 25 kids to the theater, and as I have already been saying, Shakespeare is meant to be spoken and listened to, so I recommend letting the students view the good films. As you'll see later in the book, there's no denying they make an impression on them. There are a few films I've shown over the years that I don't show anymore because they just don't get a great response from the class. They include Orson Welles' "Falstaff (Chimes at Midnight)", Kenneth Branagh's "As You Like It", Franco Zeffirelli's "Taming of the Shrew", and Laurence Olivier's

"Hamlet". They are all really good films, but they just didn't connect with my students like I wanted them to. Either too long, too slow, too cerebral, or just black and white. Normally I would fight them on the black and white thing, because I think black and white is an art form, but with Shakespeare it's about making it as easy as possible to keep their interest. Teens are a very specific audience!

TRAGEDY VS. TRAGEDY

I was listening to a podcast of the great American history professor and author Joseph J. Ellis, and he was describing slavery in America, and how it was a problem that could not be solved in 1787 as the Founders were putting together the Constitution. They kept the issue out of the document almost entirely, with the exception of adding a law to end the importation of new slaves by 1808. Ellis called slavery a tragedy, but, he added, there's a question to ask yourself- was it a Greek tragedy or a Shakespearean tragedy? That got me thinking. Did my students know the difference between Greek and Shakespearean Tragedy? I asked them. It turns out some did, some didn't. So in case the same is true with my readers, here's my quick definition: the Greek tragic characters met bad endings that were fated and inevitable, and even when they tried to steer away from it or deny it, the Gods willed it and no matter what they did, the bad ending happened. They either died, married their mother, or lost their children. Shakespearean tragic characters are brought down by their own behavior, a fatal flaw in their personality that if they could just keep it under control they'd avoid a bad ending. Of course they can't, so they kill their wives, lose the crown, or die. In short, Greek Tragedy is fate and there is nothing they can do (Oedipus), and Shakespearean Tragedy is bad choices by flawed characters that lead to a bad ending, rather than making a different choice to steer clear of it (Othello, Shylock).

Ellis, by the way, concluded the tragedy of American slavery was probably Greek, meaning there was no way to stop the inevitable Civil War. However, he added, it was better to have had the war in 1860 when the north had the best chance of winning. They probably would have lost in the 1780's. Ok, I digress, but for the sake of all the students reading this book, it's a good quick history lesson. I give those a lot in class anyway.

DID HE WRITE IT?

A question I'm asked often by students is one I know they've been hearing about and actually has been floating around scholars for the last two hundred years: "Is Shakespeare really the author of his own plays?" The rumors persist. The Earl of Oxford is the most common name thrown out by people who think Shakespeare couldn't have written such a body of work. The story goes that the educated Earl was a ghost writer for Shakespeare, and that Shakespeare himself was only an actor and then later a director/producer. He would have had so little schooling while growing up in Stratford upon Avon, that, the critics say, it would have been impossible for him to write with such an extensive vocabulary and poetic phrases. But I don't buy it. As a comparison, Mozart wrote his first symphony at the age of 4. Clearly he had only a little schooling by the age of 4. But sometimes God just hands out spectacular gifts and there's no explaining it. Mozart and Shakespeare are certainly both in that category. Plus, on a more practical note, the Earl of Oxford lived in a world that couldn't have remotely conceived of such subversive characters as Juliet, Lady MacBeth, and Falstaff. Oxford was a noble trapped in that world. I think only an actor living in the theatre backed by the Queen could get away with such characters. And, because he was an actor, Shakespeare, as I have said before, knew how to write for actors and their needs. Take his contemporary, Christopher Marlowe. Marlowe's plays are great pieces of literature, but they lack the instinctive humanity that is all over Shakespeare's plays. Shakespeare's understanding of the human condition could not be touched by Marlowe. Marlowe's plays are not as known and certainly not performed as often, and it's clear why that is. However, my answer to my students as to who wrote the plays is, I admit, very much my own opinion: *who cares*? Since it's doubtful we'll ever really know the truth, I don't waste too much time being an archeologist about it. There are those who search for any and all clues to not only authorship but also to Shakespeare's whereabouts in the late 1580's. He married Anne Hathaway in 1582, when he was 18 and she was 26 and three months pregnant! They had three children, Susanna in 1583 and the twins Hamnet and Judith in 1585. (Hamnet, by the way, died in 1596 at the age of 11, and soon after, Shakespeare wrote Twelfth Night, a story that begins with the twins Viola and Sebastian. Sebastian is thought to be drowned early in the play, but the twins reunite at the end. One can only imagine Shakespeare's heart as he wrote the reunion scene). Shakespeare disappeared from Stratford soon after the twins were born, and wound up in London writing plays and poems in 1592. No one knows for sure where he was or what he was doing during those years. There are books and documentaries on the so-called "Lost Years" but so far it's all theory. Most interestingly, his works as a whole were not published as a single volume in his lifetime. His theatre colleagues put them together and published the First Folio in 1623, a good 7 years after Shakespeare's death ("Folio", by the way, refers to the way paper was folded by printers). So all we have are the plays written by a genius who used the name William Shakespeare. Let's stay focused on that. So how exactly does one help a high school student understand a 450 year-old playwright's words? Let's get to work.

TEXT ANALYSIS

To start with, I must always reassure my students as often as possible that this material is not beyond their abilities. I promise them they will not perform their monologue until they understand every word in it, and we will not stop working on it until they do. We break down every line and look up every word they don't know and work it until they get it. So far, they always do! Every student gets a copy of all monologues so they can follow along with the students I pick to play the roles. I do scene work as well, but really to get them started on the path to understanding the Bard, I spend most of the time on monologues so they can think independently of others and also from within themselves. I always try to pick characters that fit the actors, and I also always use material that is age-appropriate. No point in having a 16 year-old attempt to understand the mind of King Lear. The sorrow of losing a child isn't, hopefully, ever in their breadth of experience. My classes average about 18 students per semester, mostly female. After trial and error over the years, here are the 18 most successful and appropriate monologues I regularly use:

ANGELO AND ISABELLA, MEASURE FOR MEASURE Act 2 scene 4
I've picked two monologues from the same play. It's a title they don't know, but it has a couple of

themes that they certainly hear every day in America- sex and politics. First thing I do is give them a quick plot summary. I don't ask them to go home and read it. For students already overloaded with college apps and regular 11th grade homework plus social life, I'm too realistic to expect them to do it. But when I start with sex and politics, these kids, who binge-watch Scandal on Netflix, get it.

The summary of Measure for Measure goes something like this: This is a play about a new sheriff in town. This guy Angelo is put in charge by the Duke who left town. Angelo enacts an old law still on the books but ignored by everyone- Pre-marital sex is a crime punishable by death. (BAM! I have their attention!) Angelo finds out Claudio, a young man in love with a girl, has been sleeping with her (turns out it's not true). So he locks him up. Claudio's sister, Isabella, who lives in a convent, meets with Angelo to plead for his release. Angelo offers up sexual blackmail instead. If she sleeps with him, he'll let Claudio go. If she doesn't, Claudio dies and dies slow. End of synopsis. Short, sweet and deadly.

Then we get to the first monologue, Angelo's blackmail speech:

ANGELO
Who will believe thee, Isabel?
My unsoil'd name, the austereness of my life,

My vouch against you and my place i'the state,
Will so your accusation overweigh,
That you shall stifle in your own report
And smell of calumny. I have begun,
And now I give my sensual race the reign:
Fit thy consent to my sharp appetite;
Lay by all nicety and prolixious blushes,
That banish what they sue for; redeem thy brother
By yielding up thy body to my will;
Or else he must not only die the death,
But thy unkindness shall his death draw out
To lingering sufferance. Answer me to-morrow,
Or, by the affection that now guides me most,
I'll prove a tyrant to him. As for you,
Say what you can, my false o'erweighs your true.

Line by line, I make sure the students understand what is being said. The first line is easy. The second is pretty easy too, but I make them look up "austereness" (they have iphones, so it takes ten seconds and they feel a part of the process). Line three we get to a whole phrase I have to work out with them "my place i'the state". He's bragging about his position in the government, namely Sheriff. I remind them not to think of the modern Sheriff in the cowboy hat and badge, but more like the Sheriff of Nottingham from the Robin Hood stories. They get that. Then I go over why the "i" has an apostrophe after it, which is to keep the line in iambic pentameter, "my place in the state" becomes "my place i'the state". Basically I tell them

to ignore the "i" and just say "my place the state".
Everyone lives with that.

It goes on like that, looking up words like "calumny"
and "prolixious", and more importantly, catching the
puns. "Fit thy consent to my sharp appetite" for
example. Yes, he said "fit". Yes it means what you
think it means when it comes to sex. I let them in on
those jokes because it humanizes the character,
the author, and reminds them nothing's changed in
400 years. Shakespeare wrote sex jokes. A lot of
them. These jokes may have gone over the heads
of the educated stuffy nobles sitting in the balcony,
but the groundlings standing up on the floor
wouldn't have missed any of them. Shakespeare
knew how to write for everyone. The more bodies
in the audience the more profit. As the students
realize that, they lose their fear of the Bard. It
works.

I also remind them that there is punctuation and to
use it. Many times they come to the end of the line
and read it like it's the end of the thought, which it
isn't most of the time. Follow the punctuation. Also
the sentences in the Angelo monologue tend to get
longer as the monologue continues. "redeem thy
brother by yielding up thy body to my will; or else
he must not only die the death, but thy unkindness
shall his death draw out to lingering sufferance."
That is one thought, and it's also a big chunk of the
second half of the speech. I ask the actor playing
Angelo what does it mean, to yield up her body?
Sex. What happens if she doesn't? Claudio must

die the death. But it gets worse. Her "unkindness" will make him suffer. I take each actor through every line until they understand exactly what they are saying. Once they get the hang of it, their comprehension speeds up. One of the true rewards of the job is when a student realizes the language is understandable. That's when teaching is most worth doing, when you see the student's world open up!

I have on occasion let them write their own modern version but I never assign it. Some need it and some don't. Some have a natural ability to understand it in their heads. Others need to write it out. Whatever works for the student. Once I get them emotionally invested, they want to succeed, and will do the work needed. That's been my experience, disregarding the one or two every semester that think all of public school is a joke. Not much we can do for them but they still have to get up and speak the speech or fail. So far, everyone has gotten up in the front of the room and done it in the five years I have taught it.

The other thing I work on with them is character. Do they know anyone like this? Are there boys right here in the school who have the moral bankruptcy to blackmail a girl into something more modern, like sending naked pictures? Is there someone famous today they want to base Angelo on? Maybe Donald Trump? Some modern rock star? The slimy professor lawyer from Legally Blonde? Lots of choices. I might also suggest perhaps the actor put on a pair of sunglasses. Or put his feet up on the desk. Maybe circle her like a vulture zeroing in on his meal. Anything to get him hooked into the dialogue on a visceral level. Angelo's a pig. We might as well bring him down into the mud and off the Shakespearean pedestal.

The next monologue is Isabella's reaction to the blackmail, same act and scene. Angelo leaves her alone in the office and she says:

ISABELLA

To whom should I complain? Did I tell this,
Who would believe me? O perilous mouths,
That bear in them one and the self-same tongue,
Either of condemnation or approof;
Bidding the law make court'sy to their will:
Hooking both right and wrong to the appetite,
To follow as it draws! I'll to my brother:
Though he hath fallen by prompture of the blood,
Yet hath he in him such a mind of honour.
That, had he twenty heads to tender down
On twenty bloody blocks, he'd yield them up,
Before his sister should her body stoop
To such abhorr'd pollution.
Then, Isabel, live chaste, and, brother, die:
More than our brother is our chastity.
I'll tell him yet of Angelo's request,
And fit his mind to death, for his soul's rest.

So now I get the actress on stage and work through it with her. Again, the first two lines are pretty easy. But what's a "perilous mouth" that bears in it one and the self same tongue? A snake maybe? Somebody two faced? Usually the actress goes with two faced. One tongue telling Claudio he must die for pre-marital sex, the other telling Isabel to sleep with him to save Claudio. He's a liar and a hypocrite. Two tongues, one face.

Then Isabella says "I'll to my brother", meaning she'll go see Claudio. Claudio will certainly die happily rather than allow his virgin convent sister to lie with this jerk Angelo. If he had twenty heads he would happily have all twenty cut off before Isabel should pollute her body with Angelo. Again, as with the actor playing Angelo, I ask the actress "have you ever been blackmailed? Did someone ever try to force you to do something?" 9 times out of 10, unfortunately, she has a personal experience she can relate to the monologue. The other students, of course, are allowed to chime in if something rings a bell. I've had a student suggest that Isabel think of her math teacher as Angelo. This actress hated math, and didn't like the teacher either, so the scene worked. The monologue concludes with Isabella's resignation that she will lose her brother but keep her chastity, which is more sacred to her. The actress usually has a hard time with that at first. "Doesn't she love her brother?" But the answer is that in that world, heaven and hell were real places and if you didn't want to go to hell, you died with honor and purity intact. I then tell the students that Claudio's reaction is quite surprising- he begs her to go through with it because he doesn't want to die! The kids react with shock! What a play Measure for Measure is!

QUEEN MARGARET, HENRY VI, P.3 Act 1 scene 4

This is one of my favorite monologues in the canon. Queen Margaret is a badass, plain and simple. The synopsis: we're in the middle of a war, called the Wars of the Roses. Her husband is hesitant to fight so she calls him spineless and signs on with the army as a general. You heard that right, a general! She and her army have defeated the Duke of York in one of the many battles of this Wars of the Roses, which was basically a civil war for the throne of England between two families, the red rose Lancasters and the white rose Yorks. ("Game of Thrones" author George R. R. Martin created the Lannister and Stark families for his novels in an obvious homage to this conflict). In this speech, right after York is captured and right before she kills him, she brutally humiliates him. Every student who gets this monologue can't believe how ruthless she is. She tears into him and never lets up. They love her!

QUEEN MARGARET

What! was it you that would be England's king?
Was't you that revell'd in our parliament,

And made a preachment of your high descent?
Where are your mess of sons to back you now?
Or, with the rest, where is your darling Rutland?
Look, York: I stain'd this napkin with the blood
That valiant Clifford, with his rapier's point,
Made issue from the bosom of the boy;
And if thine eyes can water for his death,
I give thee this to dry thy cheeks withal.
Alas poor York! but that I hate thee deadly,
I should lament thy miserable state.
I prithee, grieve, to make me merry, York.
What, hath thy fiery heart so parch'd thine entrails
That not a tear can fall for Rutland's death?
Why art thou patient, man? thou shouldst be mad;
And I, to make thee mad, do mock thee thus.
Stamp, rave, and fret, that I may sing and dance.
Thou wouldst be fee'd, I see, to make me sport:
York cannot speak, unless he wear a crown.

The first line sets the tone. York is simply not worthy to be King in Margaret's eyes. Then, at line 4, she reminds him that his sons Edward and Richard are nowhere to be found (they are still fighting) and his youngest, Rutland, was killed by the Lancastrian soldier Clifford. Margaret produces a gift: a handkerchief covered with Rutland's blood ("I stained this napkin with the blood that valiant Clifford, with his rapier's point, made issue from the bosom of the boy"). She tells York he can use it to wipe his tears. ("If thine eyes can water for his death, I give thee this to dry thy cheeks withal.") By the time Margaret mocks York by demanding he show some tears ("Stamp, rave and fret that I may sing and dance"), every actress I've asked to play Margaret gets completely involved in her antics. The final line refers to a cheap paper crown that she places on his head. Brutal, brutal stuff. I can say with certainty the students eat it up, though! They like brutal.

PRINCE HAL, HENRY IV, PART 1 Act 1 sc 2
I described part of the synopsis earlier in an earlier chapter, but here is the entirety as I would say it in class: Henry IV took the crown from Richard II, and then had him killed (that's Shakespeare's invention. Richard II actually died of starvation while imprisoned). Now Henry has enemies left and right, and he's worried that even if he can keep the crown, his son won't hold it because the prince spends his time drinking and hanging with the wrong crowd, namely the great character Sir John Falstaff and his tavern buddies. In this speech, the prince, called Hal by Falstaff, speaks an inner monologue about knowing that eventually his place will be on the throne, and he's going to have to kick these reprobates out of his life.

PRINCE HENRY
I know you all, and will awhile uphold
The unyoked humour of your idleness:
Yet herein will I imitate the sun,
Who doth permit the base contagious clouds

To smother up his beauty from the world,
That, when he please again to be himself,
Being wanted, he may be more wonder'd at,
By breaking through the foul and ugly mists
Of vapours that did seem to strangle him.
If all the year were playing holidays,
To sport would be as tedious as to work;
But when they seldom come, they wish'd for come,
And nothing pleaseth but rare accidents.
So, when this loose behavior I throw off
And pay the debt I never promised,
By how much better than my word I am,
By so much shall I falsify men's hopes;
And like bright metal on a sullen ground,
My reformation, glittering o'er my fault,
Shall show more goodly and attract more eyes
Than that which hath no foil to set it off.
I'll so offend, to make offence a skill;
Redeeming time when men think least I will.

The first line, "I know you all", is referring to his group of drinking buddies. Prince Hal puts up with their behavior at first. He will for "a while uphold the unyoked humor of your idleness." What is unyoked? One class interpreted it as an egg that loses its yolk, meaning it's run amok, like Hal's friends have all over London. Another class thought of the term "yoke of oxen", so in that case "unyoked" means the oxen have broken loose and are running wild. I like both, although since it's spelled "yoke" and not "yolk", we should go with the latter. Then Hal says he will imitate the sun. What does the sun do in this case? It "doth permit the base contagious clouds to smother up" the prince, meaning that he's hiding from his true self, and he knows it. More curiously, it appears he's doing it on purpose. He says he will be thought of as a great leader when he breaks through "the foul and ugly mists of vapour that did seem to strangle him". And when he throws off this "loose behavior", he will "falsify men's hopes", meaning his father has no hope for him, but he will prove his father wrong. His "reformation" will be "glittering o'er my fault." This is a difficult speech because the imagery is strong, but I just keep reminding the actor playing Hal that the key thought is "I will be better than this when the time comes". All high school students have had at least one moment where they weren't the best they could be, so they always relate to this character. And of course I tell them that at the end of Henry IV part two, Hal does become King and follows through on his promise, banishing old Falstaff and his buddies from his presence.

IMOGEN, CYMBELINE Act 3 scene 2
Cymbeline takes place in ancient Britain, around the time that that King Arthur movie is set, the one with Keira Knightley, when Britain is half Celtic and half Roman, probably around 300 CE. Cymbeline is King of Britain, and his daughter Imogen is in love with Leonatus Posthumus, a soldier but poor. The

King wants Imogen to marry Cloten, who's a punk if
there ever was one, a stuck up, nasty rich kid
whose mother is now the King's wife. The royals
love to keep it in the family. Imogen, just like Juliet,
refuses her father's wishes and marries
Posthumous, who is then banished from Britain and
sent to Rome. Through a series of lies and deceit,
Posthumous thinks Imogen has been unfaithful,
and sends Imogen a letter telling her to meet him in
the Welsh city of Milford Haven. The letter is
brought by Pisanio, who is Posthumous' servant,
and whom he has ordered to kill Imogen when they
get to Wales. This speech is her reaction to the
letter:

IMOGEN

O, for a horse with wings! Hear'st thou, Pisanio?
He is at Milford-Haven: read, and tell me
How far 'tis thither. If one of mean affairs
May plod it in a week, why may not I
Glide thither in a day? Then, true Pisanio,--
Who long'st, like me, to see thy lord; who long'st,--
let me bate,-but not like me--yet long'st,
But in a fainter kind:--O, not like me;
For mine's beyond beyond--say, and speak thick;
Love's counsellor should fill the bores of hearing,
To the smothering of the sense--how far it is
To this same blessed Milford: and by the way
Tell me how Wales was made so happy as
To inherit such a haven: but first of all,
How we may steal from hence, and for the gap

That we shall make in time, from our hence-going
And our return, to excuse: but first, how get hence:
Why should excuse be born or e'er begot?
We'll talk of that hereafter. Prithee, speak,
How many score of miles may we well ride
'Twixt hour and hour?

This is a wonderful speech that is playful and also
dangerous. She must defy the king, who is also
her father, and sneak out of the royal palace to go
to Wales, where's she's never been, spend time
with her husband, and get back before anyone
notices. The first line gives us the image of speed:
"O for a horse with wings!" Like Pegasus, a horse
who can fly is faster than any boat or carriage. She
asks Pisanio to read Posthumous' letter and tell her
how far it is. She knows she can move faster by
herself than any army can move in a group ("If one
of mean affairs may plod it in a week, why may not
I glide thither in a day?"). She begs Pisanio to help
her plan her secret trip, knowing he longs to see
him as much as her- well, almost! (He "long'st, but
in a fainter kind; O not like me, for mine's beyond
beyond"). She asks him for help with distance and
directions ("love's counselor should fill the bores of
hearing", the "bores" being the ears). Milford, says,
Imogen, is clearly a blessed place for keeping
Posthumous safe. She needs Pisanio's counsel to
come up with a plan and and the lie to tell her dad
about the "gap in time". Typical teenager stuff! Not
much has changed. Accept in this case, Pisanio

knows she's going to die when she gets there. But I make sure to tell the kids it will all be all right. Only the bad guys die in this play.

PUCK, A MIDSUMMER NIGHT'S DREAM Act 3 scene 2
This play is one of the Big 5, but Puck is too good a character not to include him. The plot is complex with all those different interacting stories- the lovers, the mechanicals, the faeries, and the court at Athens, so I just stick to Puck's role. Puck, also known as Robin Goodfellow, is an immortal servant to Oberon, the king of their faerie world. Puck is playful, philosophical, and thoroughly whimsical. Oberon's wife, Queen Titania, is having a quarrel with the King over a boy she stole from him to live among her servants. Jealous Oberon asks Puck to find a flower that contains a potion to make the victim fall in love with next person he/she sees. Puck uses the flower on the young human lovers who are chasing each other all over the forest, but also on Titania while she's sleeping. The first person she sees when she wakes is Bottom the weaver, an actor whose head Puck has transformed into one of a jackass. Why? Because Bottom is kind of a jackass, an ego-driven narcissist who is rehearsing a play with the mechanicals and wants to play every part himself. This is Puck's description of Bottom's transformation and Titania's waking moment!

PUCK
My mistress with a monster is in love.
Near to her close and consecrated bower,
While she was in her dull and sleeping hour,
A crew of patches, rude mechanicals,
That work for bread upon Athenian stalls,
Were met together to rehearse a play
Intended for great Theseus' nuptial-day.
The shallowest thick-skin of that barren sort,
Who Pyramus presented, in their sport
Forsook his scene and enter'd in a brake
When I did him at this advantage take,
An ass's nole I fixed on his head:
Anon his Thisbe must be answered,
And forth my mimic comes. When they him spy,
As wild geese that the creeping fowler eye,
Or russet-pated choughs, many in sort,
Rising and cawing at the gun's report,
Sever themselves and madly sweep the sky,
So, at his sight, away his fellows fly;
And, at our stamp, here o'er and o'er one falls;
He murder cries and help from Athens calls.
Their sense thus weak, lost with their fears
thus strong,
Made senseless things begin to do them wrong;
For briers and thorns at their apparel snatch;
Some sleeves, some hats, from yielders all
things catch.
I led them on in this distracted fear,
And left sweet Pyramus translated there:
When in that moment, so it came to pass,

Titania waked and straightway loved an ass.

So we start off with the result- Titania loves the asshead Bottom. Then Puck backtracks to the beginning and describes in detail how we got here. But before we go further, notice something special about this dialogue- it's in rhyming couplets. So, in fact, is most of the play! Thats right, the majority of the whole damn play rhymes the first line with the second. It's AB almost all the way through. That Shakespeare was a genius.

Back to Puck's story- he basically retells the previous scene, so it's interesting that Shakespeare makes Puck share with Oberon what the audience already knows. Now he has to work twice as hard to keep it interesting. First, Titania was sleeping, then the Mechanicals start rehearsing, and Puck turns Bottom, whom he describes as "the shallowest thick skin of that barren sort", into a half human half donkey monster. When the Mechanicals see him, "away his fellows fly"!

But then Titania waked, and "straightway loved an ass." The students love that last line!

LADY ANNE, RICHARD III Act 1 scene 2
One of my favorites and a true classic is King Richard III. Richard's deformity is exaggerated to show how evil and corrupted he is. He's called horrible names by everyone in the play (half the lines from that Shakespeare Insults t-shirt is from Richard III), and Lady Anne is no exception. Lady

Anne's husband, a Lancaster, was killed by
Richard, a York, and he also killed Anne's father in
law, Henry. In this scene, Henry's body is being
taken to his burial when Richard stops the
procession, which was a very disrespectful thing to
do back then. You just don't ask the men to lay
down the shrouded body to have a talk with a girl.
It's bad taste. But Lady Anne takes the opportunity
to let him have it.

LADY ANNE

*Foul devil, for God's sake, hence, and trouble us
not;*
For thou hast made the happy earth thy hell,
Fill'd it with cursing cries and deep exclaims.
If thou delight to view thy heinous deeds,
Behold this pattern of thy butcheries.
O, gentlemen, see, see! dead Henry's wounds
Open their congeal'd mouths and bleed afresh!
Blush, Blush, thou lump of foul deformity;
For 'tis thy presence that exhales this blood
From cold and empty veins, where no blood dwells;
Thy deed, inhuman and unnatural,
Provokes this deluge most unnatural.
*O God, which this blood madest, revenge his
death!*
*O earth, which this blood drink'st revenge his
death!*
*Either heaven with lightning strike the
murderer dead,*
Or earth, gape open wide and eat him quick,

As thou dost swallow up this good king's blood
Which his hell-govern'd arm hath butchered!

Anne minces no words. "Foul Devil" is the first line in her speech and first thing she calls him. Pretty intense. While she's giving him his tongue lashing, Shakespeare gets all supernatural on her. The body of Henry starts to bleed. Dead bodies don't bleed, but here "dead Henry's wounds open their congealed mouths and bleed afresh". She says "blush", which means "feel some shame for your behavior", and then call him a "lump of foul deformity". Obviously Anne thinks he has it coming, and so would the audience, since Queen Elizabeth is the granddaughter of the man who defeated Richard at Bosworth in 1485. The audience better be on her side for this obvious piece of propaganda that favors the beginning of the Tudor family line and the end of the Plantagenet line. Anne concludes the speech with a double curse- either heaven strike him dead or the earth eat him. The girls love playing Anne!

AARON, TITUS ANDRONICUS Act 2 sc 3
Titus is like no other play in the canon. Violent, ugly, and full of horrible characters, this play was a hit because, as I tell my students, it's a Saw film, and the Saw films make money. If you've never seen a Saw film, it's all blood, gore and violent deaths, and young people love that stuff. Shakespeare's audiences in the early 1590s loved

this one. The plot is simple enough- the Roman general Titus Andronicus has returned from conquering the Goths. He brings back some high profile prisoners, like Tamora, the Queen of the Goths, her servant Aaron, a Moor, and her oldest son, whom Titus promptly orders killed. Tamora plots revenge, and with the help of Aaron, they arrange for Tamora's remaining two sons to jump Titus' daughter and her fiance in the forest. They will kill him, rape her, and then cut off her hands, cut out her tongue, and leave her there. The kids' response is usually "what ever happened to Romeo and Juliet?", and my response to that: "I haven't even gotten to the part where Titus kills the two boys who raped his daughter and cooks their bodies in a pie which he then serves to their mother and then they all kill each other in the final scene." Yeah, that's right- Shakespeare, the boring love sonnet guy, wrote Titus Andronicus with a Sweeney Todd ending. BAM!

Anyway, this speech belongs to Aaron, the servant, who lets Tamora know while the two of them are alone what he has planned for her sons and Titus' daughter.

AARON

Madam, though Venus govern your desires,
Saturn is dominator over mine:
What signifies my deadly-standing eye,
My silence and my cloudy melancholy,
My fleece of woolly hair that now uncurls

Even as an adder when she doth unroll
To do some fatal execution?
No, madam, these are no venereal signs:
Vengeance is in my heart, death in my hand,
Blood and revenge are hammering in my head.
Hark Tamora, the empress of my soul,
Which never hopes more heaven than rests in thee,
This is the day of doom for Bassianus:
His Philomel must lose her tongue to-day,
Thy sons make pillage of her chastity
And wash their hands in Bassianus' blood.
Seest thou this letter? take it up, I pray thee,
And give the king this fatal plotted scroll.
Now question me no more; we are espied;
Here comes a parcel of our hopeful booty,
Which dreads not yet their lives' destruction.

When the speech begins, Tamora has just asked
Aaron to lay with her in the biblical way. But in his
first line, he makes it clear that he's not in the
mood. Venus, the goddess of love, may be on
Tamora's mind, but Saturn, the god who killed his
children, is on Aaron's. He makes a slight
reference to his blackness ("my fleece of woolly
hair that now uncurls"), but otherwise he's a straight
ahead villain. He lets Tamora know his thoughts
are not "venereal", but instead all about vengeance.
Bassisanus, the fiance of Titus' daughter, will die
today, he says. And his "Philomel" will lose her
tongue (Philomel was a character in Greek
Mythology who was also raped and mutilated), after

the boys "pillage her chastity", which means cold blooded rape. He then mentions a letter to give to the king that frames Titus' sons for Bassianus' murder. Then they must stop talking because someone is nearby. It's Bassianus, the "parcel of our hopeful booty". He has minutes to live. My students laugh at "booty", but I remind them that booty in the old days meant stolen goods. They laugh anyway.

ANTONY, JULIUS CAESAR Act 3 scene 2
This is from the same scene as the famous "Friends, Romans, Countrymen lend me your ears" speech, but I use this lesser known monologue because the other is too (in)famous and makes the kids giggle. They giggle often enough. The short version of this true story: Julius Caesar ruled at the very beginning of the Common Era. His assassination by Roman senators Brutus, Cassius, Casca, and 9 others in 44 AD became the basis for Shakespeare's play of betrayal and politics. Brutus, the lead conspirator, was a close friend of Caesar, so Shakespeare gives Caesar the famous final words "Et tu, Brute?"("You too, Brutus?") While being stabbed by Brutus and the other senators, Caesar is shocked to learn his friend had turned on him. After Caesar's death, Brutus makes a speech to the citizens of Rome who have gathered in front of the senate building. He declares that what he did was righteous, because Julius Caesar was a tyrant. Then he leaves. Marc Antony, a young general who

knew both Caesar and Brutus well, assures Brutus he will back his coup d'etat. Then Antony gives a speech, and it turns the crowd against Brutus.

ANTONY

If you have tears, prepare to shed them now.
You all do know this mantle: I remember
The first time ever Caesar put it on;
'Twas on a summer's evening, in his tent,
That day he overcame the Nervii:
Look, in this place ran Cassius' dagger through:
See what a rent the envious Casca made:
Through this the well-beloved Brutus stabb'd;
And as he pluck'd his cursed steel away,
Mark how the blood of Caesar follow'd it,
As rushing out of doors, to be resolved
If Brutus so unkindly knock'd, or no;
For Brutus, as you know, was Caesar's angel:
Judge, O you gods, how dearly Caesar loved him!
This was the most unkindest cut of all;
For when the noble Caesar saw him stab,
Ingratitude, more strong than traitors' arms,
Quite vanquish'd him: then burst his mighty heart;
And, in his mantle muffling up his face,
Even at the base of Pompey's statua,
Which all the while ran blood, great Caesar fell.
O, what a fall was there, my countrymen!
Then I, and you, and all of us fell down,
Whilst bloody treason flourish'd over us.
O, now you weep; and, I perceive, you feel
The dint of pity: these are gracious drops.

Kind souls, what, weep you when you but behold
Our Caesar's vesture wounded? Look you here,
Here is himself, marr'd, as you see, with traitors.

Antony begins by holding the bloody cloth, called a
mantle, that Caesar was wearing. (In the film
version with Marlon Brando as Antony, Brando
carries out the entire body. But for the sake of a
lack of a body in my classroom, the cloth works just
as well.) His opening line changes the mood from
cheering to somber. He reminisces on the cloak
and on Caesar's greatness. Then he points out
each hole now in it, from the stabbings, and
corresponds an assassin's name with each hole.
That's a good way to turn the crowd against the
assassins, to make Caesar a human victim.
Shakespeare gives Antony beautiful and haunting
imagery of the stabbing ("mark how the blood of
Caesar followed it, as rushing out of doors, to be
resolved if Brutus so unkindly knocked"), and
shows Brutus to be the traitor and betrayer of his
friend Caesar ("This was the most unkindest cut of
all; For when the noble Caesar saw him stab,
Ingratitude, more strong than traitors' arms,
Quite vanquish'd him"). Antony keeps it up for the
rest of the speech, emotionally recalling Caesar's
fall and naming Brutus as a traitor ("Kind souls,
what, weep you when you but behold
Our Caesar's vesture wounded? Look you here,
Here is himself, marr'd, as you see, with traitors").
By the time he's done, the crowd turns on Brutus,

who is then hunted by Antony's army for the rest of the play.

PORTIA, JULIUS CAESAR Act 2 scene 1
Here's another great monologue from Julius Caesar. Earlier in the play, before the death of Caesar, it's clear to Brutus' wife Portia that something is going on that's not kosher. Brutus is preoccupied, uneasy, and he refuses to talk to her about it. Like any good wife, Portia demands her right to know what's going on.

PORTIA
Is Brutus sick? and is it physical
To walk unbraced and suck up the humours
Of the dank morning? What, is Brutus sick,
And will he steal out of his wholesome bed,
To dare the vile contagion of the night
And tempt the rheumy and unpurged air
To add unto his sickness? No, my Brutus;
You have some sick offence within your mind,
Which, by the right and virtue of my place,
I ought to know of: and, upon my knees,
I charm you, by my once-commended beauty,
By all your vows of love and that great vow
Which did incorporate and make us one,
That you unfold to me, yourself, your half,
Why you are heavy, and what men to-night
Have had to resort to you: for here have been
Some six or seven, who did hide their faces
Even from darkness.

Within the bond of marriage, tell me, Brutus,
Is it excepted I should know no secrets
That appertain to you? Am I yourself
But, as it were, in sort or limitation,
To keep with you at meals, comfort your bed,
And talk to you sometimes? Dwell I but in the
suburbs
Of your good pleasure? If it be no more,
Portia is Brutus' harlot, not his wife.

When the speech begins, Brutus is on his way out.
Portia tries several tactics to get Brutus to talk. In
the first few lines, she mothers him. It's cold out,
she tells him, you might be getting sick, so you
shouldn't go out without a coat. Don't be outside,
away from your warm bed, in the middle of the
night, when there's germs out there. Then she
switches gears, and accuses him of being sick in
the head ("No my Brutus, you have some sick
offense within your mind"). After that doesn't work,
she begs him and plays on his recent lack of
affection ("and on my knees, I charm you, by my
once commended beauty"), then reminds him of
their promise at their wedding to communicate ("By
all your vows of love and that great vow which did
incorporate and make us one, that you unfold to
me, yourself, your half, why you are heavy"), and
then accuses him of hanging around with
suspicious men that "did hide their faces even from
darkness". Finally, she rages against a wife's role
in marriage ("Portia is Brutus' harlot, not his wife"),

in a very contemporary understanding, I might add, of women's ancient outdated roles in society. This speech holds up with young women very well!

JULIET, ROMEO & JULIET Act 4 scene 3
So now we get to the most famous teenager in theatre. I know I said I'd stay away from the Big 5, but I already broke that rule with Puck, and this is a great speech! Juliet is alone in her room, her marriage to Paris arranged, Romeo sent word (she thinks) to come to the tomb and get her out, and she's holding the vial she has to drink to fake her death. So, like anyone who's about to roll the dice on the rest of their life, she sits there wondering if all of this is a good idea.

JULIET
How if, when I am laid into the tomb,
I wake before the time that Romeo
Come to redeem me? there's a fearful point!
Shall I not, then, be stifled in the vault,
To whose foul mouth no healthsome air breathes in,
And there die strangled ere my Romeo comes?
Or, if I live, is it not very like,
The horrible conceit of death and night,
Together with the terror of the place,--
As in a vault, an ancient receptacle,
Where, for these many hundred years, the bones
Of all my buried ancestors are packed:
Where bloody Tybalt, yet but green in earth,

Lies festering in his shroud; where, as they say,
At some hours in the night spirits resort;--
Alack, alack, is it not like that I,
So early waking, what with loathsome smells,
And shrieks like mandrakes' torn out of the earth,
That living mortals, hearing them, run mad:--
O, if I wake, shall I not be distraught,
Environed with all these hideous fears?
And madly play with my forefather's joints?
And pluck the mangled Tybalt from his shroud?
And, in this rage, with some great kinsman's bone,
As with a club, dash out my desperate brains?
O, look! methinks I see my cousin's ghost
Seeking out Romeo, that did spit his body
Upon a rapier's point: stay, Tybalt, stay!
Romeo, I come! this do I drink to thee.

Right off the bat, it's clear the tomb itself is creeping her out. In those days the dead would have been put in the family vault, an underground building with stone tables to put the dead on, covered with nothing more than a cloth shroud. So she would have woken up surrounded by, as she says,"the bones of all my buried ancestors are packed". Cousin Tybalt was killed the day before, so he's freshly laid out, and not looking too good, and there's a good chance the newest dead are in the same area. She might wake up next to him. That's on her mind as well ("where bloody Tybalt, yet but green in earth, lies festering in his shroud"). Then she talks herself into waking up with ghosts and spirits and noises and shrieks all around her, and how she'll probably lose her mind if that happens, and beat herself with someone's thigh bone ("with some great kinsman's bone, as with a club, dash out my desperate brains"). The monologue ends with her thinking she's seeing Tybalt's ghost right there in the room, and she screams "Stay Tybalt, stay!", meaning "stay where you are, don't come any closer!" Finally she toasts Romeo and drinks the drug. The students guess she drinks it to shut up her own brain. I agree.

HERMIONE, THE WINTER'S TALE Act 3 scene 2
The Winter's Tale is a wonderful late play that makes up for Othello's bloody conclusion by presenting a conclusion of redemption and forgiveness. King Leontes is so jealous of his Queen Hermione for hanging out with the Duke who lives nearby, that he has her arrested. Despite the fact that there is even less direct evidence than in Othello (no handkerchief in this one), the King refuses to let her see their newborn son, not even to breastfeed him, and drags her in front of a crowded judge's chamber to call her a whore in public. They even use an oracle from Apollo's temple (basically a guy who meditates on the signs and evidence and concludes what is the truth). Hermione, of course, is just a good person surrounded by proud men, and an idiot for a husband. Here at the trial, she speaks to the King,

right after he proclaims that a guilty verdict means death:

HERMIONE
Sir, spare your threats:
The bug which you would fright me with I seek.
To me can life be no commodity:
The crown and comfort of my life, your favour,
I do give lost; for I do feel it gone,
But know not how it went. My second joy
And first-fruits of my body, from his presence
I am barr'd, like one infectious. My third comfort
Starr'd most unluckily, is from my breast,
The innocent milk in its most innocent mouth,
Haled out to murder: myself on every post
Proclaimed a strumpet: with immodest hatred
The child-bed privilege denied, which 'longs
To women of all fashion; lastly, hurried
Here to this place, i' the open air, before
I have got strength of limit. Now, my liege,
Tell me what blessings I have here alive,
That I should fear to die? Therefore proceed.
But yet hear this: mistake me not; no life,
I prize it not a straw, but for mine honour,
Which I would free, if I shall be condemn'd
Upon surmises, all proofs sleeping else
But what your jealousies awake, I tell you
'Tis rigor and not law. Your honours all,
I do refer me to the oracle:
Apollo be my judge!

From the beginning, she knows the trial is rigged, and she's already lost. The king will influence the verdict and no one will dare challenge him, so she's already dead. She says as much, and on top of that, welcomes death. ("The bug which you would fright me with I seek.") Then she lists the three things that make her life no longer worth living- the king has lost favor with her ("I do feel it gone, but know not how it went"), she can't see her son ("first fruits of my body, from his presence I am barr'd"), and she can't breastfeed ("the innocent milk in its most innocent mouth, haled out to murder"). Finally, she throws in that he's put her on public display to slut-shame her ("Myself on every post proclaimed a strumpet"). So let's get on with it, she says. But, she adds, "I shall be condemn'd upon surmises, all proofs sleeping else but what your jealousies awake. I tell you 'tis rigor and not law." In other words, "be careful, you made all this up in your own jealous head, and it is not civil, it is cruel." And as a parting shot, she asks for the oracle to be read. The oracle, of course, proclaims her as innocent. But Leontes, being no better than Othello, ignores the oracle, like Andrew Jackson did when he completely ignored the United States' Supreme Court in the 1838 Georgia v Cherokees decision. (The court pronounced the Cherokees sovereign and allowed to stay on their land, but Jackson sent in the army anyway, and the Cherokees were forced in winter weather to march the Trail of Tears to Oklahoma. A quarter of them died on the way.)

Unlike the Cherokees, however, Hermione gets a
chance to fake her own death, which snaps
Leontes into reality, leading to the forgiveness
scene in the final act, which takes place 16 years
later! The Winter's Tale is an extraordinary play!

LADY MACBETH, MACBETH Act 1 scene 5
So now we come to the Lady herself. This is
another character all the women in my class love to
play. Most lay people know the wife of MacBeth as
the driving force behind the murders, and of course
for that "out damned spot" speech. In this
monologue, we get to see just how human she
really is, as she stands there terrified, but still
determined that the murder of Duncan must be
carried out.

LADY MACBETH
The raven himself is hoarse
That croaks the fatal entrance of Duncan
Under my battlements. Come, you spirits
That tend on mortal thoughts, unsex me here,
And fill me from the crown to the toe top-full
Of direst cruelty! make thick my blood;
Stop up the access and passage to remorse,
That no compunctious visitings of nature
Shake my fell purpose, nor keep peace between
The effect and it! Come to my woman's breasts,
And take my milk for gall, you murdering ministers,
Wherever in your sightless substances
You wait on nature's mischief! Come, thick night,

And pall thee in the dunnest smoke of hell,
That my keen knife see not the wound it makes,
Nor heaven peep through the blanket of the dark,
To cry 'Hold, hold!'

As we all know from reading "The Raven" by my homeboy Edgar Allan Poe, ravens were messengers of death. This speech starts off hearing a hoarse raven, who has been crowing all night, warning of Duncan's death. Creepy and awesome! Then she starts praying to the spirits of the night to "unsex" her, which means make her not as a woman but as a man, one who is filled from the "crown to the toe, top-full of direst cruelty". Then she demands the night spirits to make her blood thick, which will keep her from feeling remorse, and for these evil apparitions in the dark to drink her breast milk filled with impudence. Next she asks Night itself to use its darkness to cover her so she can not see what she is doing, and also so heaven and her conscience cannot see her doing it and try to stop her! This guy Shakespeare could write.

JOAN OF ARC, HENRY VI PART 1 Act 1 scene 2
History lesson on Joan of Arc- a French shepherd girl during the 100 Years War with England gets a vision from the Virgin Mary, who tells her to stop farming and to take up the sword against the enemy. This 15 year-old girl, in the year 1420, winds up not only asking the future King of France

if she can be a general in the army, but is granted the request, and kicks some ass in the Battle of Orleans. Henry VI is king of England during all this. Although eventually captured, tried as a witch and burned at the stake, Joan's achievements cannot be overlooked. She was found innocent of heresy in 1456 and canonized a Saint in 1920. In this speech, she begs the Dauphin, the heir to the throne of France, for a chance to fight in the war.

JOAN LA PUCELLE
Dauphin, I am by birth a shepherd's daughter,
My wit untrain'd in any kind of art.
Heaven and our Lady gracious hath it pleased
To shine on my contemptible estate:
Lo, whilst I waited on my tender lambs,
And to sun's parching heat display'd my cheeks,
God's mother deigned to appear to me
And in a vision full of majesty
Will'd me to leave my base vocation
And free my country from calamity:
Her aid she promised and assured success:
In complete glory she reveal'd herself;
And, whereas I was black and swart before,
With those clear rays which she infused on me
That beauty am I bless'd with which you see.
Ask me what question thou canst possible,
And I will answer unpremeditated:
My courage try by combat, if thou darest,
And thou shalt find that I exceed my sex.
Resolve on this, thou shalt be fortunate,

If thou receive me for thy warlike mate.

This one is pretty straight forward until line 5, then it gets more complicated. In short, she's saying that while tending sheep in the hot son, the Virgin Mary ("God's mother") appeared and said to put down the shepherd staff and fight in the war! ("And in a vision full of majesty will'd me to leave my base vocation and free my country from calamity".) Then we have an interesting, old-fashioned view of beauty: "whereas I was black and swart before......that beauty am I bless'd with which you see". In other words, being out the in sun made her tan, but since she saw Mary, her skin got pale. All the paintings of the period show paleness as the epitome of what was attractive. Then Joan lays out her resume: she's smart, and she can fight ("Ask me what question thou canst.......my courage try by combat"). And her last two lines make it clear that she's telling the Dauphin that saying yes would be a good move ("Thou shalt be fortunate if thou receive me for thy warlike mate"). Another great female character for the class to enjoy!

VIOLA, TWELFTH NIGHT Act 2 scene 2
For anyone who has seen "Shakespeare in Love", you'll remember that Viola dresses like a boy to be near the man she loves, who happens to be William Shakespeare, the poet, playwright and sometimes actor. The movie ends with him writing the play Twelfth Night. I only mention that because the

movie is so damn good! Anyway, in the play, Viola dresses like a boy to be close to Duke Orsino. The Duke, however, is trying to win the heart of Olivia, who wants nothing to do with him. Orsino sends Viola to talk Olivia into it. Olivia falls in love with Viola instead. Is everything clear? Excellent. On her way back from Olivia's house, Viola is chased down by Olivia's servant, who gives Viola a ring from Olivia. It becomes clear in the speech that follows that Viola realizes Olivia fell in love with the wrong guy!

VIOLA

I left no ring with her: what means this lady?
Fortune forbid my outside have not charm'd her!
She made good view of me; indeed, so much,
That sure methought her eyes had lost her tongue,
For she did speak in starts distractedly.
She loves me, sure; the cunning of her passion
Invites me in this churlish messenger.
None of my lord's ring! why, he sent her none.
I am the man: if it be so, as 'tis,
Poor lady, she were better love a dream.
Disguise, I see, thou art a wickedness,
Wherein the pregnant enemy does much.
How easy is it for the proper-false
In women's waxen hearts to set their forms!
Alas, our frailty is the cause, not we!
For such as we are made of, such we be.
How will this fadge? my master loves her dearly;
And I, poor monster, fond as much on him;

And she, mistaken, seems to dote on me.
What will become of this? As I am man,
My state is desperate for my master's love;
As I am woman,--now alas the day!--
What thriftless sighs shall poor Olivia breathe!
O time! thou must untangle this, not I;
It is too hard a knot for me to untie!

There are many possibilities of exactly the moment Viola realizes Olivia loves her. It could be the line "She loves me". Or maybe "I am the man". But I think it's earlier in the speech, as soon as the second line "Fortune forbid my outside have not charm'd her". If you play it that way, the rest is confirmation: Olivia was staring at her, speaking erratically, used the messenger to give her this ring, yep it's clear! But then Viola makes it even more clear she doesn't bat for that team ("poor lady, she were better love a dream"), and waxes philosophical about being in disguise and a woman's easily malleable heart. After that it's a plot summary ("How will this fadge? ['Fadge' means 'to resolve'] my master loves her dearly; and I, poor monster, fond as much on him; and she, mistaken, seems to dote on me"). It's all to remind Shakespeare's audience just how silly this whole thing is, but if we just stick around, it will all work out!

HELENA, ALL'S WELL THAT ENDS WELL Act 3 scene 2

Helena is a character that many young people can relate to- she loves someone who doesn't love her. That's all I need to tell them. Her husband, who was forced to marry her, has no plans on being faithful or even caring. He's off to the Tuscan wars and sends her home without a goodbye kiss. Helena later intercepts a letter from her husband which makes clear his plans to seduce all the local virgins while pretending his wife doesn't exist. The letter includes the line "til I have no wife, I have nothing in France." This is Helena's response:

HELENA

'Till I have no wife, I have nothing in France.'
Nothing in France, until he has no wife!
Thou shalt have none, Rousillon, none in France;
Then hast thou all again. Poor lord! is't I
That chase thee from thy country and expose
Those tender limbs of thine to the event
Of the none-sparing war? and is it I
That drive thee from the sportive court, where thou
Wast shot at with fair eyes, to be the mark
Of smoky muskets? O you leaden messengers,
That ride upon the violent speed of fire,
Fly with false aim; move the still-peering air,
That sings with piercing; do not touch my lord.
Whoever shoots at him, I set him there;
Whoever charges on his forward breast,
I am the caitiff that do hold him to't;
And, though I kill him not, I am the cause
His death was so effected: better 'twere

I met the ravin lion when he roar'd
With sharp constraint of hunger; better 'twere
That all the miseries which nature owes
Were mine at once. No, come thou home,
Rousillon,
Whence honour but of danger wins a scar,
As oft it loses all: I will be gone;
My being here it is that holds thee hence:
Shall I stay here to do't? no, no, although
The air of paradise did fan the house
And angels officed all: I will be gone,
That pitiful rumour may report my flight,
To consolate thine ear. Come, night; end, day!
For with the dark, poor thief, I'll steal away.

Helena blames herself for his leaving to fight in the war, and also prays for his safety. It might seem pathetic, but it's also very human. We've all cared about people who don't care about us, whether it's right or wrong. Anyway, the first line repeats the line in the letter, and then she reacts by planning to grant his request. But then her tone changes. She knows she's the cause of him leaving (is't I that chase thee from thy country and expose those tender limbs of thine to the event of the none-sparing war), and will not forgive herself if he gets hurt. Her description of war-employed musket balls is one of my favorite pieces of writing in Shakespeare's entire canon: "O you leaden messengers, that ride upon the violent speed of fire, fly with false aim; move the still-peering air,

that sings with piercing; do not touch my lord."
Wow.
She then goes back to blaming herself ("Whoever
shoots at him, I set him there"), and then decides
she will leave him to make him happy ("I will be
gone, that pitiful rumour may report my flight, to
consolate thine ear"). It's basically the same theme
as Dolly Parton's "I Will Always Love You". I just
have to get out of teaching before a student asks
"who's Dolly Parton"? I won't be able to handle it.

PROTEUS, TWO GENTLEMEN OF VERONA Act
3 scene 1
This is one of Shakespeare's earliest plays, some
scholars say it's the very first, and it's a pretty
simple straightforward comedy- two guys, one girl.
Valentine is in love with Sylvia, and his friend
Proteus, also in love with Sylvia, tries to stop
Valentine. The end.
In this speech, Proteus knows that Valentine is
going to break Sylvia out of her locked bedroom
and elope with her, so he runs to the Duke, her
father, to rat him out.

PROTEUS
My gracious lord, that which I would discover
The law of friendship bids me to conceal;
But when I call to mind your gracious favours
Done to me, undeserving as I am,
My duty pricks me on to utter that
Which else no worldly good should draw from me.

Know, worthy prince, Sir Valentine, my friend,
This night intends to steal away your daughter:
Myself am one made privy to the plot.
I know you have determined to bestow her
On Thurio, whom your gentle daughter hates;
And should she thus be stol'n away from you,
It would be much vexation to your age.
Thus, for my duty's sake, I rather chose
To cross my friend in his intended drift
Than, by concealing it, heap on your head
A pack of sorrows which would press you down,
Being unprevented, to your timeless grave.

I direct my actor playing Proteus to be over the top frantic with this speech. The comedy, in my opinion, is in the exaggeration of the event! Proteus tells the Duke he has some information which surely the Duke needs to hear- Valentine "this night intends to steal away your daughter"! Since the Duke has arranged for Sylvia to marry some guy named Thurio, Proteus reminds the Duke that he's old and this elopement would raise his blood pressure considerably ("And should she thus be stol'n away from you, it would be much vexation to your age").

I like to hold off introducing this monologue until we have gone through several other more difficult ones, because Proteus' language is fairly straightforward and simple, given that it's one of Shakespeare's first plays. That way, the students are always surprised at how easy this speech is to understand, and so their confidence rises!

JAQUES, AS YOU LIKE IT Act 2 scene 7
Yes, I know, this is one of the more famous speeches in the canon, but the truth is most people only know the first line, with a few more knowing the first two lines. The entire speech, I've discovered, is still pretty unknown to a teenage audience so it's fair game in my opinion. The first thing we have to do is get past the English butchering of his French name. Every production I've seen of As You Like It calls him "jay-queez". So I do, too. The students laugh, but they'll get past it. Jaques is the most famous cynic of Shakespeare's characters, more so than his Fool characters because of this very speech. It's a brutally nihilistic view of the world.

JAQUES
All the world's a stage,
And all the men and women merely players:
They have their exits and their entrances;
And one man in his time plays many parts,
His acts being seven ages. At first the infant,
Mewling and puking in the nurse's arms.
And then the whining school-boy, with his satchel
And shining morning face, creeping like snail
Unwillingly to school. And then the lover,
Sighing like furnace, with a woeful ballad
Made to his mistress' eyebrow. Then a soldier,

Full of strange oaths and bearded like the pard,
Jealous in honour, sudden and quick in quarrel,
Seeking the bubble reputation
Even in the cannon's mouth. And then the justice,
In fair round belly with good capon lined,
With eyes severe and beard of formal cut,
Full of wise saws and modern instances;
And so he plays his part. The sixth age shifts
Into the lean and slipper'd pantaloon,
With spectacles on nose and pouch on side,
His youthful hose, well saved, a world too wide
For his shrunk shank; and his big manly voice,
Turning again toward childish treble, pipes
And whistles in his sound. Last scene of all,
That ends this strange eventful history,
Is second childishness and mere oblivion,
Sans teeth, sans eyes, sans taste, sans everything.

First off, Jaques calls all people actors. From Shakespeare's time all the way up to the birth of Hollywood fan magazines, actors were considered some of the lowest forms of human life around. Of course, all the Hollywood fan magazines did was polish a turd, but that's another book to write. Jaques then goes through the famous seven stages of man, starting with the infant "mewling and puking in the nurse's arms". The school boy is next followed by the lover, the soldier, the judge, the old man (the "pantaloon" is a stock character in Commedia D'ell Arte, old, skinny and bespectacled), and finally the senile, infirm, fragile elder, not long for this world. Jaques ends this "strange eventful history" as man's history must end, with death, which he calls "mere oblivion". What a wonderful ironic phrase. There's nothing casual about oblivion, but he uses the word "mere". Wicked writing. Then there's the word "Sans", which is French for "without", so death is not only the end of sight and taste, but of everything. No afterlife, no Heaven, just nothing. Shakespeare's society had strong Catholic roots, so this would have been blasphemy. But Shakespeare was, once again, bold.

CIPHERS TO THIS GREAT ACCOMPT

I've been asked multiple times by students over the years- do I have a single favorite Shakespeare monologue? Actually I do, and I'll never assign it because the character shows up in only a few scenes and only talks to the audience. It's the Prologue by the Chorus from Henry V. Why? It's really good writing! The prologue is spoken by an actor who is not playing a role, which is unusual for Shakespeare. He's just an actor from the company guiding you through this play. The thing I like best, however, is that he is encouraging the audience to think like film editors, before there was such a thing! Jump cuts, giant on-location sets, dissolves and wipes, what we all know to be film vocabulary, were things that Shakespeare was trying to write for the theatre. Henry V starts in England, cuts to

Southampton and a boat launch across the
channel, cuts to the French King and his court, cuts
back to Henry landing and marching to Agincourt,
capturing Harfleur along the way, cuts back to the
French court, and then cuts to the battle on October
25, 1415 with 20,000 Frenchmen and maybe 9,000
Englishmen. The scale of it is incredibly cinematic,
and here's the Chorus telling the audience to
forgive all for not being able to put it on stage, but
to please pretend it was!

CHORUS

O for a Muse of fire, that would ascend
The brightest heaven of invention,
A kingdom for a stage, princes to act
And monarchs to behold the swelling scene!
Then should the warlike Harry, like himself,
Assume the port of Mars; and at his heels,
Leash'd in like hounds, should famine, sword and
fire
Crouch for employment. But pardon, and gentles
all,
The flat unraised spirits that have dared
On this unworthy scaffold to bring forth
So great an object: can this cockpit hold
The vasty fields of France? or may we cram
Within this wooden O the very casques
That did affright the air at Agincourt?
O, pardon! since a crooked figure may
Attest in little place a million;
And let us, ciphers to this great accompt,

On your imaginary forces work.
Suppose within the girdle of these walls
Are now confined two mighty monarchies,
Whose high upreared and abutting fronts
The perilous narrow ocean parts asunder:
Piece out our imperfections with your thoughts;
Into a thousand parts divide on man,
And make imaginary puissance;
Think when we talk of horses, that you see them
Printing their proud hoofs i' the receiving earth;
For 'tis your thoughts that now must deck our kings,
Carry them here and there; jumping o'er times,
Turning the accomplishment of many years
Into an hour-glass: for the which supply,
Admit me Chorus to this history;
Who prologue-like your humble patience pray,
Gently to hear, kindly to judge, our play.

The speech opens with a prayer for inspiration and
imagination: to fill the stage with a kingdom, full of
princes and monarchs, and Harry! He's the warrior
king, sailing from the port of Mars, the God of War,
with the instruments of battle by his side! Then
suddenly, the monologue changes course and
apologizes for pretty much failing to provide on
stage what was just described. We're just actors,
the Chorus says, and we suck, but we're going to
do our best and we need your help to fill in the
blanks with your imagination. Then he says "since a
crooked figure may attest in little place a million",
meaning please think of one person on stage as a

million people, so you'll be able to enjoy the battle scenes. Another great line from the prologue is "Think when we talk of horses, that you see them Printing their proud hoofs i' the receiving earth; For 'tis your thoughts that now must deck our kings". In other words, "you guys won't see any horses tonight, but I really hope you imagine they're there." The prologue is a contract, a bond between audience and performers that we're all in it, together, to create the magic of theatre. It doesn't get much more real than that for us artists. I love this piece. One day I'll play the Chorus. One day....

DON'T KNOW MUCH ABOUT HISTORY
The worlds that Shakespeare created were not fantasy worlds, with a few exceptions (the Faery World in A Midsummer Night's Dream and Prospero's Island in The Tempest, for example). They were either contemporary or historical times, which means I as a teacher have to do the research to make sure the students understand the world these plays are in. I've been a fan of American history all my life, but since I started studying Shakespeare I have done a lot of research on English monarchies. It helps to have that background when I teach the Bard. I have a lecture in the first few days about the Tudor dynasty, beginning with Richard III's defeat at Bosworth in 1485 by Henry VII, a Tudor. I emphasise the need for male heirs to keep the current family on the

throne. If Henry didn't have sons to inherit the throne, any number of others could stake a claim to England based on the family trees of either the Lancasters and Yorks. That's what happens when you take the crown by force. Luckily Henry had two sons, Arthur and Henry. Arthur died young, but his brother Henry became the famous Henry VIII. I then take the students through the six wives of Henry VIII, beginning with Catherine of Aragon, the daughter of Ferdinand and Isabella of Spain, who was married to Arthur before he died, and then became Henry's wife. Only one daughter survived infancy, Mary. Henry believed marrying his brother's wife may have cursed him, plus he was falling hard for Anne Boleyn. Catherine's refusal to accept divorce caused the break with Rome and the formation of Church of England. (Remember though, that Mary is Catherine's daughter, and therefore was raised Catholic.) Henry marries Anne Boleyn, but they also only have a daughter, Elizabeth. Anne is also not well liked by the English commoners because they are still secretly Catholic and did love Catherine as their Queen. Meanwhile, Henry is falling for Jane Seymour, who was one Anne's attendants. Henry had Anne Boleyn arrested on a trumped up charge of adultery with her own brother, and then executed her in 1536, which then freed Henry to marry Jane. They had a son, Edward, so finally Henry has his heir, but Jane died in childbirth. Henry then married three more times. Anne of Cleves was an arranged marriage that Henry claimed was never consummated, and divorced her immediately. Catherine Howard was much younger than Henry, and was caught cheating on him, and executed. His final wife was Catherine Parr, who outlived him. Henry passed a law restoring Mary and Elizabeth to the line of succession, after Edward. He certainly didn't think Edward would only live to be 15, so Mary indeed got to the throne. Mary I, known as "Bloody Mary", brought back her mother's Catholicism to England, and was burning Protestants at the stake left and right, earning her nickname. She married Spain's King Philip II, but they had no children and she died of stomach cancer in 1558, making it another short reign on England's throne. So against all odds, Elizabeth I, one of the greatest monarchs in English history, reigned for 45 years. Elizabeth and her love of theatre brought William Shakespeare to the scene; he was in his prime as a writer during Elizabeth's years. Scottish King James I was next on the throne in 1603, and Shakespeare retired in 1610, during James' reign. Jamestown and the colony of Virginia happened in 1607, which was within Shakespeare's lifetime. I always mention that in my history lecture because it connects us Americans to Shakespeare in the timeline of history, which the students don't usually realize. But why do I do a history lecture in a Shakespeare class? Because it's important for the students to know the world he was writing in. It was a dangerous world, where the wrong material or character could be considered subversive or treasonous and Shakespeare might have wound up in prison or executed. He had to pick his material carefully and push boundaries as much as he could without going too far. Again, he was lucky Elizabeth liked theatre, for he may not have written so boldly without her. This entire lecture only takes one class. But I'm happy to say I have their attention the whole time, and the indication for me is when I announce the death of Jane Seymour, the gasps and groans are audible, every semester!

A quick word on the history plays, as they're called. They are a group of plays about the previous Kings of England. Most take place during the Wars of the Roses, a period ripe with drama for the stage. The history plays were incredibly popular money makers during Shakespeare's career. I personally love the history plays, so monologues from Henry V and Richard III are common in my classroom.

And of course, the year 2012 produced, in my opinion, the greatest archeological find in my lifetime so far (with the possible exception of the discovery of the wreck of the Titanic in 1985): the grave of King Richard III. My students don't normally read about world news, so it was my pleasure to break the story to them! My class watched this happen in real time. I kept giving them updates as the news got to me. To recap, Richard was killed at the Battle of Bosworth field in 1485 by Henry Tudor, later crowned King Henry VII. He was quickly buried in a nearby church, but no one today knew where the church was. A team of excavators thought they had discovered the right location beneath a parking lot in Leicester, in the north of England. As they began to dig, they discovered, on the first day, a human skeleton with several wounds and a curved back. Word of a direct descendant of Richard's sister Anne led the team to a carpenter from Canada, living in England, who did a DNA test and confirmed the skeleton was the former King of England and famous Shakespearean villain! The following year, I shared the reburial footage of King Richard III. In a coffin built by his carpenter descendant, Richard was ceremoniously rode through Bosworth field before being laid to rest at Leicester Cathedral in 2015, 530 years after his death. The students were quite riveted, and what they enjoyed the most was the facial reconstruction of Richard's skull, and the study of the weapons that killed him. On a side note: researchers also recently reenacted a battle sequence from that period with a young man with scoliosis, to see if he could ride and fight in the armor. What they discovered was that the young man rode just fine, but tired quickly on foot because of issues with lung capacity. Richard's fatal decision at Bosworth, it would appear, was to get off his horse. So suddenly, Richard's final lines in Shakespeare's play mean even more now than they ever did before: "A horse! A horse! My kingdom for a horse!" So there you have it. Ten years after teaching my first acting class at OCSA, 12 years after my graduation from California Institute of the Arts, and nearly 40 years since my brother Steven's 5th grade production of Romeo & Juliet, I can scratch "write a book" off my Bucket List. I conclude with this final thought: this book was written by a fan of both the Bard and the teenage mind's true ability to grasp the material. Shakespeare did not just write his works for the rich, upper class, stuffy nobles; he wrote for the masses. So to me it is completely wrong that we treat his works as if they're rich, upper class, stuffy plays. He wrote for you and I, for the common man and woman, for the humanity in us all. He wrote to hold the mirror up to nature, so that we can see ourselves in these characters and learn from them. My sincerest wish is that this book will release teachers and students alike from their fears, and to help in the understanding of the immeasurable value in bringing Shakespeare to the new Millennium. His works are of the people, by the people, and for the people, and they should not be allowed to perish from the earth.

OCSA CONFESSIONS
I asked my former students from the Orange County School of the Arts to send me a paragraph or two of whatever stood out in their minds from my Shakespeare classes. The results encouraged me to write this book. Here are some of my favorites:

Kaytra Parkman

I clearly remember the day when you finally talked REALISTICALLY about Shakespeare. You explained to us not every single word is as "sacred" as some teachers make it out to be. You pointed out the humor, the historical references, and what was just plain nonsense. By showing that it was imperfect, I started resisting it less, because now I felt like it was being taught more genuinely.

I hate when people put anything on a pedestal. So the different ways you went about teaching Shakespeare, from explaining the history of the time to the sexual innuendos, made it MUCH more accessible to a young person.

I liked how you went about the acting portion as if it were just regular dialogue, and made it more real. That once we grasped what it was about, we could "speak" it normally, instead of TRYING to make it sound "Shakespeare".

Jessica Lincoln

What I learned was that Shakespeare was no different than people and society today. You broke it down for us when we were making it seem as if reading and comprehending Shakespeare was like breaking the laws of gravity, when really it was pretty simple and similar to the latest celebrity gossip or even high school drama. You made it much clearer to understand and see that Shakespeare would mention societal issues as well and when you would make the comparison, I didn't feel like a train wreck reading it anymore; I was definitely more appreciative of the beautiful text than I was before.

Amanda Godoy
You inspired a curiosity and eventual love for Shakespeare that I didn't think I had. I used to only think of myself as a tap dancing musical theatre actress, but you made the Bard relevant and easy to access and understand, and it made me realize that I was more capable of acting than I thought possible, if that makes sense. Now I'm studying straight stage and film acting, and my first college production was Shakespeare based. Thank you so much for your teaching!

Sydney Pardo
I find so few are able to understand that absurd, erudite stuff Shakespeare wrote, and our English teachers rarely help. We read through R & J without understanding half of what is said, only skimming old English words from a paperback book. I was never taught the historical context in school, the Tudor Era or the Wars of the Roses (until your class), nor did we spend time discussing why the themes persist to this day. No one says why we should study Hamlet, just that we should. Frankly, we are set up to dislike the Bard's work in such a learning environment where we are forced to read and analyze but not understand or care.

Tom Palmer
Watching the movie Shakespeare in Love gave me a new appreciation for Romeo and Juliet. Even though it was fiction, the idea of real love and romance influencing a play about love and romance is profound to me. The end of Romeo and Juliet especially has a new place in my heart. Not because of love or romance, but because of the depression that he felt after having lost her. I personally relate to that more, than the idea of killing yourself out of love.

Kelly Zhou
As opposed to analyzing miniscule nuances in language as we had done in previous literature classes, we examined larger themes and discovered the true meaning behind why we call Shakespeare's work universal. It is quite difficult to look at the big picture and how the pieces apply to our lives when we need to annotate every instance of assonance to death!

Nina Brandon
I learned that Shakespeare is not as hard to read and understand as people say. If you break the text down piece by piece it doesn't feel as difficult and now I feel confident that I can take on other Shakespeare works and understand ones that I watch.

Jovi Nieto

Something that really sunk in for me was when we discussed Shakespeare's depiction of women and the way he portrayed them throughout his plays. Especially that time, it's really surprising that such strong, bold and rebellious characters in his plays were often female. Even now it's rare that women characters in movies are portrayed as independent, strong, smart, and admirable people. Usually they are pretty and kind and smart, but they are dependent on or revolving around a man. Shakespeare's women are beautiful. They are smart. They are rebellious and don't conform to society's expectations and standards. Most importantly, they are POWERFUL! This fascinated me and I continue to learn from Shakespeare's women as a young woman myself, even though they're about 400 years older than me!

Nirvana Shahriar
The main thing that helped me understand Shakespeare was actually acting out the scenes because it forces you to understand the characters' motivations and emotions behind the words, which helps in understanding the words.
(Author's note: Nirvana started out in 9th grade with "No Fear Shakespeare" in her backpack. After taking my class she discovered a love for it, deep enough to spend a college semester in England studying Shakespeare at Oxford!)

Lea Garn

Now that I've taken this class, it's amazing to see
how many Shakespeare plays/motifs are in modern
popular culture and media.

Tennessee Mills
My favorite thing about your class was transcribing
the text. Re-writing each line in a modern syntax
was ridiculously helpful. And also fun!

Hannah McMullen
Reading was never my thing. Being born dyslexic
made reading to a group of my peers humiliating or
just slow. So a class where I was almost positive
that that was what we'd be doing made me a little
afraid. But Mr. Schwadron delivered. He used his
background in acting to help us truly interpret
Shakespeare's words, and made it feel less like a
popcorn session in some boring literature class and
more like a rehearsal for our version of the play.
Once I put myself in that mindset, reading aloud
was less of a pain and more of a pleasure. He
taught us how speak and read Shakespeare's
unique language to where I now consider myself
fluent.

Lilah Azizadah
Literature class is so focused on dissecting the text.
It also limits the realm of Shakespeare to very few
plays. This class broadened my knowledge of other
less popular plays and helped me learn to
appreciate the text in a new way.

Isabel Ronquillo
I discovered that learning the language of
Shakespeare's time is really not difficult if you
break it down, phrase by phrase, and dive into the
content.

Nicole Carcerano
When you showed us Joss Whedon's Much Ado
About Nothing, my opinion of the whole class
changed. That's when all of a sudden I loved it and
realized that no matter how old the subject, it still is
relevant to our problems that we choose to gush
over daily. Shakespeare somehow wrote stories
where the women were real and they had emotions
and they expressed them, even when it was
repetitive. I mean, we are repetitive naturally as
humans; he just wrote what I felt was real, and his
writing transcends time.

Acknowledgements:
Thanks to Marilyn Schwadron, Steven Schwadron, Acela Pena, Marissa Chibas, Arthur Horowitz, Travis Preston, Fran Bennett, Joan MacIntosh, Rocco Sisto, Mike Davies, Michael Levine, Shannon Leclercq Allen, Heather Stafford, Sean McMullen, William Wallace, Chris Dion, Jeff Paul, Kathleen Whitlock, Colleen Happ, Kathy Brown, Jennifer Rennels-Magon, Jymn Magon, Victoria Goodman, PBS, OCSA, Cal Arts, CSU Northridge, Canyon Theatre Guild, The Poxy Boggards, and The Original Renaissance Pleasure Faire.

Cover photo by Phil Schwadron
Author's photo by Adriana Reza-Harris

About the Author:

For over 40 years, Philip Schwadron has been involved in the performing arts as an actor, director, dancer, singer, songwriter, playwright and musician. He began his professional career at the age of 13, performing in the 1983 Tony Award-winning Broadway production of ON YOUR TOES. After moving to Los Angeles, Philip, along with his twin brother Steven, acted professionally in television (CHEERS, BEVERLY HILLS 90210) and film (SAFE PASSAGE, THE APPLEGATES). Philip received his BA in Theatre Arts from CSU Northridge, followed by his MFA in Acting from California Institute of the Arts.

Currently, the Schwadron brothers write songs, record, and perform with the vocal comedy group The Poxy Boggards. They also perform and record as 2/3 of a folk trio called Three of A Kind.

Philip teaches Shakespeare Appreciation for 11th grade and Acting for the Camera for 10th grade in the Integrated Arts Department at the Orange County School of the Arts. He has worked in IA at OCSA since 2007, teaching Acting and Tap Dancing as well, plus Acting Techniques for the OCSA Music and Theatre department. This is his first book.